I0458387

Poetic Anarchy

Copyright ©2025 Gregory Cioffi. All rights reserved.

No part of this book may be reproduced in any manner whatsoever without written permission except in the case of brief quotations embodied in critical articles and reviews.

NO AI TRAINING: Without in any way limiting the author's and Henry Gray Publishing's exclusive rights under copyright, any use of this publication to "train" generative artificial intelligence (AI) technologies to generate text or images is expressly prohibited. The author reserves all rights to license use of this work for generative AI training and development of machine learning language models.

For information, contact: henrygraypub2022@gmail.com

Publisher's Cataloging-in-Publication Data

Names: Cioffi, Gregory, 1987- .
Title: Poetic Anarchy / Gregory Cioffi.
Description: Granada Hills, CA : Henry Gray Publishing, 2025.
Identifiers: LCCN 2025922695 |ISBN 9781960415646 (hardback) | ISBN
    9781960415622 (pbk.) | | ISBN 9781960415639 (ebook)
Subjects: LCSH: American poetry—21st century. | Experimental poetry,
    American. | Rebellion in literature. | Freedom—Poetry. | Art and
    society—Poetry.
Classification: LCC PS3603.I65 P64 2025 | DDC 811/.6—dc23
LC record available at https://lccn.loc.gov/2025922695

Cover © 2025 Diego Garcia. All Rights Reserved.

Made in the United States of America.

Published by Henry Gray Publishing
17020 Chatsworth Blvd. #1125, Granada Hills, California 91344

For more information or to join our mailing list,
visit HenryGrayPublishing.com

Poetic Anarchy

Gregory Cioffi

HENRY GRAY
HG
PUBLISHING

Granada Hills, CA
"Select books for selective readers"

Also by Gregory Cioffi

Novels

THE DEVIL IN THE DIAMOND

Poetry Chapbooks

SUMMER HEAT: POEMS OF PASSION

THE DIVINE TRAGEDY

A STRANGE AFFINITY

"I believe that artists are the vanguard of the species. That is the last chance that we have of connecting as human beings. The music, the paintings, and so forth. And once those run out of gas, then we're at the end of the republic."

— *Cornel West*

Whatever your love language is, Gregory Cioffi will ravish you in **Poetic Anarchy.** This collection is philosophical, erudite, erotic, and, despite its title, masterfully constructed. With nods to Dickinson, Whitman, and Ginsberg, Cioffi seduces the reader with food, art, and, my personal favorite: social justice. Cioffi's range is astounding. All of history's famous lovers gather here. Dante and Beatrice share space with Gomez and Morticia. But the biggest turn-on in these poems is self-discovery. Provocative, playful, and soulful, this work will woo you with defiance and passion. It will prime you to perceive that there "are potential connections everywhere," and that is something to swoon over.

—Deborah Hauser
Author, *Ennui: From the Diagnostic and Statistical Field Guide of Feminine Disorders* (Finishing Line Press); Poet Laureate, Suffolk County, NY (2023-2025)

Poetic Anarchy by Gregory Cioffi is a journey through contemporary poetry. Searching with questions, observations, insights and descriptions, he weaves a tapestry of poems using poetic devices, form and style, following rules and breaking them with purpose. Mr. Cioffi doesn't just paint pictures with words but creates snapshots that focus sharply on or blur the conception of reality with exposure, using contrast and color, but sometimes blunt in black and white to express his views on his inner-self, society, day to day life and poetry in general. Living in an age of cynicism, he asks, "What's next in the art of poetry?" Read **Poetic Anarchy** and it will provoke you into deep thought both emotionally and intellectually.

—Peter V. Dugan
Nassau County Poet Laureate 2017-19

Throughout the pages of **Poetic Anarchy** Gregory Cioffi invites you on a journey exploring a windfall of emotion in a world of social suspicion. The poet packs a punch with expressive language and striking imagery in both traditional and brilliant contemporary forms. In the *Gehenna* poems, Cioffi evokes a Dantean pilgrimage into the afterlife; and in *Roller Coaster Ride* you will ride-the-read to the final freefall. I encourage you to pace your path through the well-crafted landscape of **Poetic Anarchy** and engage in the emphasis of existence. Cioffi adds, "If you were to declare it time to leave/I would without question, beg/Plug me back in."

—Robert Savino
Suffolk County Poet Laureate 2015-2017

Author's Note

Thank you. Thank you for taking the time out of your significant and valuable lives to read my first full volume of poetry. It is the ultimate criterion through which one can measure whether or not these words are still alive. So I suppose you are actively (and hopefully enthusiastically) participating in my immortality. Thanks. I appreciate that.

But let's get to the obvious question. What do I mean by *Poetic Anarchy?*

I am not advocating for the political removal of institutions or rulers. I know. Some of you are disappointed already. I am, however, taking a deep delve into disorder and contesting the history of artistic authority and acceptance. Many "rules" are altered or outright broken. And yet some, of course (to remain truly anarchistic), are pristine examples of tradition. Here you will find closed form/fixed form poetry coinciding with open form and free verse in harmony. This harmony exists with the only through-line being a sort of creative lawlessness. Sensual love poems could be followed by pieces with the spark and spirit of revolution, which might just be followed by an ode to chicken cutlets. You never know. And that's the point.

Admittedly, not every poem I ever wrote is in this collection (though every poem I ever published up to this point is included). Some just didn't make the cut for one reason or another. However, there are poems here that are some of the first I ever wrote. True juvenilia. Some of these pieces I grouped with the overarching title of *Adolescent Thoughts* and they are juxtaposed by very new pieces that are clearly superior by every imaginative standard. But does that make those teenage word doodles truly less valuable? What does it mean when those pieces sit side by side with pieces far more complex? I am often surprised when I submit numerous poems to an upcoming anthology, and I mix much older work with new work, that the older work has a pretty successful track record. Perhaps I don't see myself in those pieces any longer. But perhaps someone else does. Who knows, maybe that someone is you. I am not the arbiter of artistic value and so I shall give you all of it. This questioning and objection to hierarchy is also *Poetic Anarchy*.

Lastly, I believe art is dangerous. It is why the artists are usually one of the first groups to be silenced in times of turmoil. Art can be a disruption of the status quo, a challenge to some ordered ideal. Above all, art presents new possibilities and realities that are perhaps not as beyond our reach as some would like you to believe.

This collection of utterances I call *Poetic Anarchy* is meant to be a journey. One where you have absolutely no idea what is to follow on the unexplored next page. So hop in. Go for the ride. You don't even have to wear a safety belt. No restraining devices necessary.

What could possibly happen?

The Silent Poet

The poet is silent
Not because the poet has nothing to say
But because the poet knows not what to say
Or perhaps
How to say it

And so the poet retreats inwards
To reflect
Meditate
And ponder
Leaving the outside world without words

But rest assured
The poet will return
And rise with fervor
And the poet shall thunder
With passion and piety
With seriousness and sincerity
With excitement
And enthusiasm

For the poet knows
Art is a needed bastion
For any pursuit of truth and compassion

And so very soon
The Poet will be silent
No longer

Poetic Anarchy

Death to conformity, stand your own ground
I believe they say rules were meant to break
Give birth to freedom for this has no bound
Shatter the shackles and your own path take!

Uniqueness: A radical thought indeed!

Poetry without authority – a state of
    lawlessness
Obliterate masculine and feminine scansion
    – watch me transgress!

Take verbs and nouns
Interchange them at will!
Creativity?

wrong so is this that say to you are Who
along play I'll smart so you're think You

They say free verse allows for unrestricted
    writing
Thanks Walt!

Death to the strophe, antistrophe and epode
Break the bindings
And liberate yourself – control this episode

This is my invitation to a new originative
    nation
Murder your hesitation and live on
    inspiration
Experience the fruitfulness of creative
    innovation
And allow yourself to come to the literary
    revelation

Welcome to poetic tranquility
Welcome to poetic anarchy…

F
   R
     E
       E
      D
    O
M

P.S. I'm entitling my haiku and senryū…

Manifesto

Too long have we compromised our dear arts!
The time has come! Hear my declaration!
When the money invades, the art departs
This has pushed this artist to frustration

A creative fission has taken place!
A wrongful, blasphemous, fragmentation!
Craft has been removed – surely a disgrace
What I will do is my obligation

Entertainment and skill must be combined!
Intellect breeds the imagination
Now allow me to free the confined mind
Welcome to my artistic salvation!

It is time to again turn on the lights
It is time for art to regain its rights!

I See the Minds of My Generation...

I see the minds of my generation as a societal severance
A split world of various *style*
I *see* most have been **STRUCK** with the <u>Pale</u> **<u>Fist</u>** of ignorance
Dwelling in their own misguided understanding of human nature
Unwilling to see beyond.
The Others have fOrced their Optical lids tO Open
And see the world and its function
This group understands because they WaaaaaNT to
They stray from the malicious ways
The wretched expectations
And the societal norms
Not to be radical but simply because they see no other way
The others, however, give in to the ways of TREND and f

a
l
l
victim

To the **TERROR** of detrimental **compliance**
The violent fusion builds and clouds judgment
Dispersing and extracting many from my youth
This is why this generation has so few enLIGHTened.
The empty
The weak
And the closed-minded
Have been pulled
And confiscated
By the most demonic abstraction in existence
... blindness ...

This Poem of Mine

this poem of mine
what is it?

is it a mere byproduct
of the awareness
of my mortality?

a challenge
to my own fear
of death?

if so
will it succeed?
will this poem outlive me?
allow me the opportunity
to deny annihilation?

perhaps more importantly
is it why I do it?

if five minutes ago
before I sat down to write this
I knew the universe would end tonight
would I write this?

if no one ever read it
or even had the chance to read it
would I scribe it?

this poem of mine
what is it?

they say poetry
is an exercise
in patience, passion, and perseverance
but maybe
it's all just an exercise
in outlasting demise

do I fear being forgotten?
I do
do I hope my work survives me?
I do

But why?

this poem of mine
what is it?

perhaps
it is not so much
that death is inevitable
but rather
that it is unpredictable
that has me up at odd hours of the night
penning poetic self-preservations
as I repel the ever-expanding
taunts of terror

what do I do
now that I realize
I have created
simply as a means
to produce something
meaningful enough
to counter biological reality itself?

well
it's quite simple really
I shall take my fear
and cherish it
for it allows me
the convenience
to finish
this poem of mine

Annihilationism

The Last Judgment proved to be a very long line
Of course no one complained, you know, to seem benign

Herb twiddled his thumbs but was in no rush
He pondered the 72 virgins thing and this made him blush

He peered ahead and could make out an aiding disciple
Looking around, amidst clouds, all seemed pretty archetypal

Soon Herb could see, front and center, his savior Jesus Christ
He regretted once flipping out over turkey that was overpriced

It was eventually his turn and he apprehensively looked up
"So? Can I drink from the Holy Grail? The chalice? The cup?"

Jesus looked him up and down as if programmed
And then stated, "Says here you are damned."

"Damned!? I can't be damned! I don't want to go to Hell!"
Herb protested as anxiety began to quell

"Be calm and do not worry.
Hell doesn't exist," he said in a hurry.

"It doesn't!? That was all fiction?
Wow. Such pains to develop its depiction.

So what does this mean? Where do I go?
Most importantly, do they serve espresso?"

"Those who annoyed
Shall simply be destroyed."

"Whoa! The heavenly guillotine!
What, by that, do you actually mean?"

"Your consciousness will be extinguished
Your existence will be eternally undistinguished."

"Whoa! Eternal torment is sounding pretty good right now.
What about that commandment? You shall…not kill…thou?"

Herb was hoping to acquit
But Jesus wasn't taking any shit

Thinking quickly, Herb sought a loophole
"What about my immortal soul?"

The Son of God could sense some strife.
"Not given until you are granted eternal life.

He annihilates those who lived with immorality
Leaving only the righteous to live on in immortality.

The wicked He shall then justly cremate."
"Great. No Hell. Just going to eviscerate."

"Fear not. There will be no torment.
But you must go, as sins you did not repent."

"I repented! I repent all the time! I repent right now!
How can this happen!? I was an upstanding citizen! How!?"

"This is a testament. You're a self-saboteur.
You are incompatible with God's holy character."

"Some character. Sounds a bit like a hypocrite.
So. Okay. I guess then that this is it?"

Jesus nodded with a degree of stoicism
Awaiting the impending annihilationism

"Just answer me one thing for my own affirmation
Was it all the excessive masterba

First published in *All The Men Came & Danced*

THE MOST ASTOUNDING FACT

The man said looking up at the night sky
He feels not at all small, but rather big
For the stars are there to cosmically verify
An excavation of truth if you dig

Every atom in our body can be traced
To the melting pots of light which birthed stars
Collapsed, exploded, their entrails were spaced
Across galaxies, spreading heavenly memoirs

Life's ingredients formed system upon system
Generation after generation
Spawning beautiful galactic mayhem
And we, humankind, are that culmination

Look up, all is not disconnected and thus
Grasp! The universe itself is within us!

First published in the 2021 chapbook *A Strange Affinity*

Star Children

I would like to add another thing
that is sure to excite

Since every atom in us formed
from an exploding sun

The atoms in your left hand came
from a different star
    than your right!

First published in the 2021 chapbook *A Strange Affinity*

Full Bodied

A bottle of red acts as the radius
Between us
We each have a glass
And a yearning to quench
A certain thirst

And so we swirl
And sip
And savor
In service
Of this full bodied foreplay

We relish in its sweetness
Become willfully trapped
In its web of viscosity
Delight in that oily sensation
In the middle of your tongue

Most are unaware
That it's actually the acidity
Which makes the mouth water

With each sample an inhibition
Falls by the wayside
With each swallow
Blood flows and fills
While erogenous zones flood

The body describes
How it feels in the mouth
And so suffice it to say
It is most certainly
Full bodied

But it's the tannin of titillation
Appealingly astringent and bitter
That stimulates balance
And provides structure to the experience

Supple spirits
Arousing aromas
Liquid pleasures abound
Uplifting thrusts of unseemliness
Break leafless laws of indecency
For which I very much plead guilty

I pluck the grapes of your vast vineyard
And entirely enjoy your particular variety
For you are the vintner of vehemence
And most exceptionally vintage

Well-balanced and complex
You evolved beautifully over time
With a smooth texture
And a rich flavor
The ritual of romance
Holds seductively strong
As we consume without moderation
The magic moments of life

Through exquisiteness itself
And sensory satisfaction
I became intoxicated
As we finished making love on the kitchen table

First published in *Summer Heat: Poems of Passion* (2025)

The Celestial Dictator

It watches you while you sleep

Its rule cannot be challenged
And Its eternal reign may not be disputed

It denies you the privilege of freedom
It says you cannot be moral without It
It convicts you of thought crime
It is Totalitarianism incarnate

It needs you to fear It
It needs you to love that which you fear
It is the essence of sadomasochism
It is the master-slave relationship
It believes it has rights on your life
It demands that it owns you
It wants you to be proud of your chains
It eagerly awaits your demise

As Its ownership of you only begins at death.

It is evil

First published in the 2022 chapbook *The Divine Tragedy*

Kisses and Conversation

Our coupling
A cyclical recapitulation
Of kisses and conversation

Our thoughts
An ever-probing
Intellectual libation
Our lips
A hard day's work
A longing vocation
Our words
Free unbound ideas
A thoughtful temptation
Our touch
Unrestricted trust
A sensory salvation
Our communication
All lines open
Word dancing flirtation

Our quivers
Electric ecstasy
A shocking salutation
Our listening
In the moment
Without mental migration
Our tongues
Uniting
In carnal captivation
Our seesaw
Listen. Respond.
Endless fascination
Our kisses
Hungers quenched
From sensual starvation
Our conversations
Arousal incarnate
Cerebral aspiration

Our coupling
A cyclical recapitulation
Of kisses and conversation

First published in *Summer Heat: Poems of Passion*

RainboWS WiTHOUT Rain

Is it truly impossible to see
Rainbows without rain?
Hope stems from the storm, we decree
Is it truly impossible to see
Beauty without debris?
I wonder, as I look out my windowpane,
Is it truly impossible to see
Rainbows without rain?

First published in 2023 by *The RavensPerch*

One of Two, Tertiary Adjunct of Unimatrix Zero One Love

He who was once one
Met her
She who was once one
Met him

An assimilation of adoration transpired

Together the two
Became singular
The metaphoric one flesh
Emotionally, spiritually, and intellectually linked
A symbiotic hive mind
A Collective of Two
One unit. One couple
A shared identity

But in the end their love proved futile
As Two of Two severed their lengthy connection

One of Two
He who was once one
Was abruptly torn away
And found himself
In disarray
Disoriented by forced individuality

In his head
Existed the solace and support of dual voices
But now
There was only his own

With the "we" now "I"
And the "our" now "my"
They tell him he's liberated

But really
He just feels
Incomplete

First published in *The Scene,* Issue #8, January 2024

This Age of Cynicism

In this Age of Cynicism
I grow weary of the world

Where any effort for virtuosity
Is met with hostility

Are you naïve or part of the swindle?

Have you fallen victim to the scam of compassion?
The shakedown of altruism?
The sham of generosity?

Anyone claiming otherwise is sanctimonious!
Self-righteous drivel
Under the guise of good

Are you too weary of this world?

A world where decency is a mere attempt
At virtue signaling?

A world of
Constant questioning!
Constant doubt!
Constant apprehension!
As we actively seek out
...ulterior motives...

We have become cold
Untrusting
Suspicious and skeptical

And so
What should we do?

Revel in our selfishness without apology
Or
Question our social responsibility

In this Age of Cynicism

Gregory Cioffi

THE SEARCH FOR MY OTHER SELF

Who am *I* find it astonishing how one event can have
    such an impact
That it everlastingly alters the self
One **emotional,** unforgettable happening *molds* us
Forces us to sPliT; triggers a *fragmentation*
Now, you see, there is more than one me
I have another self – a **steppenwolf**!

I am now a soldier dashing across love's battlefield
I build defenses to protect myself [let no one in!]
And am getting accustomed to this **cold, emotionless** life

I trust only this me

Who was *I* once knew nothing of this struggle
Call me naïve, call me ignorant – but it was **bliss**
Peace and harmony dominated my one self

The attack was unexpected and thus, the aftermath unthinkable
I had no training for ***This* armed conflict just smacked me
    in the face**
And now neither words nor actions can harm this **unmoved man**

A forced *fission* changes you, *you know* I am wounded
Forever b*leeding* but never succumbing
Day after day I fight life's strife
Looking for victory and my old self
For the true defeat would be to stay in this war zone!

So who am *I*?

Simply a shell-shocked soldier
Seeking serenity

Friday Night Ritual

Like clockwork
Every seven days
A chair is pulled out
And wine is poured in
Pre-set glasses
Set upon
An unblemished
Tidy tablecloth
That will soon become
Quite blemished
The appetizing aroma
Drives into the dining room
As the oven is opened
And the meal upon
The baking sheet
Checked

Smooth jazz melodies
Mumble messages
Of wordless warmth
In our heated home

The square tray
With the sizzling
Sustenance
Is set down
A culinary centerpiece
Ogled and awed at

The cutter slices
Up our anticipation
As the vigorous strokes
Shake the table
The full wine glasses
Dance in chaos
As some crimson liquid
Inescapably escapes
And crashes upon
The once unblemished
Tidy Tablecloth

Death to linen disinfection

After serious deliberation
The first slices are disseminated
And we raise our glasses
In a shared cheers
To good health

Some nights
The spinach sparkles
Other nights
The mushrooms mouth-water
Ricotta dabs
Add a delectable delicacy
Pepperoni progresses
Sausage assuages
And
There is nothing plain
About a plain pie

A golden-brown hue
Signifies a perfectly done
Dough

That first bite
Is all you need to know
The level of perfection
Coupled with another sip
A life fulfilled

An evening excellently spent
A ritual that I wish
Never reaches resolution

For Friday is perfection
And so too is the paragon
Pizza

First published in *Pizza Poems*

IT'S ALL GREEK TO RATIONAL THOUGHT

If all is designed, much seems treasonable
But there's an old choice in divine acumen
What about those twelve unreasonable
Gods who didn't pretend *not* to be human?

They sat on Mount Olympus in appetite
They were secretive and surreptitious
Not at all all-beneficent and polite
Instead they embraced the capricious

At least they would be understandable
When pondering our imperfect affairs
At least our minds could prove expandable
When thinking about what goes on upstairs

What if the Greeks played a sacred scrimmage?
What if we really are made in *their* image?

First published in the 2022 chapbook *The Divine Tragedy*

ODE TO SHITTY DINER COFFEE

The rain pours outside the diner's glass window
As I delay getting back on the metro

I sit in the overheated respite
Waiting for my clothes to dry just a bit

The booth is both soft and satisfying
Foamed vinyl seats always prove gratifying

And then it comes – steaming from the counter
On a tray; with the waitress, an encounter

She places it down on the worn table
My hands reach out, once shaking but now stable

They wrap around that classic plain white mug
Preparing to experience the caffeinated drug

My body is warmed before the first sip
I pick it up and bring it to my lip

I slurp it in while hoping for delight
But you never quite know on such a night

Taste the inexpensive over-roasted beans
Pondering cleanliness behind the scenes

I swallow the coarse black liquid turmoil
The type that can only stem from rancid oil

It's a little weak and has that day-old taste
No doubt placed atop a burner to ease waste

It took me mere moments to finish the blend
That had surely been sitting for hours on end

The waitress returned and asked, "A refill?"
I nodded and she could glean my sincere thrill

The coffee was hot and the diner moonlit
"Yes please, it's perfect, just how I like it."

"Huh. That's odd. Most people say it's shitty."
"Those people, I think, we should probably pity."

She looked befuddled yet still rather pretty
I drank and turned to look at my city

In a shifting world with countless exchanges
I hope this diner coffee never changes

First published in *The Scene* Issue #20, March 2025

The Interlocking

It first occurs in the desirous eyes
        A sparkle that shall sensationalize

        Heads cock and unhurriedly gravitate
Anon, pairs of flesh yearningly conjugate

The integration is unremitting
        Emotions amorously transmitting

        Tools for tasting pierce the pulpy blockade
Greet each other; agreeably invade

The quivering interlocking then slows
        Pull away; the moment comes to a close

        If a picture does hold a thousand words
And a city contains limitless herds

Then what is a kiss but a new frontier
        A universe of pleasure to revere

        For when time and space bear little meaning
A vacuum exists; holds naught but feeling

First published in *PAUMANOK: Interwoven*

Love Verboten

Envisage a passion so strong
A coupling of depraved lovers
Whose fierce commitment is lifelong;
Extends beyond spouses covers

This love transcends all social norms;
Conventional morality
Prevails against wuthering storms
And immune to finality

They're unlike foliage of woods
Which is chewed by time's passing teeth
Retreat home to durable goods;
They're the eternal rocks beneath

They exist beyond the last breath
They love in spirit after death

First published in *PAUMANOK: Interwoven*

SONDER

I stop at the corner and look up
Into dozens of illuminated windows
At a myriad of lives
Through framed glimpses

I ponder how each individual above
Has a full complex life
As complex as my own
And how they drive the narratives
Of their realities

Is she a lawyer?
Or a librarian?
Is he an actor?
Or an accountant?

What feuds are fueling?
Which romances revving?
Who might be mourning?
Which feelings are forming?

Why does she type so seriously?
Why is he showering so?
Why are you debating between shirts?
When the one on the left is the way to go

Do they know we can see them?
Making love against the glass?
Of course they do
They decided en masse

That one watches baseball on a big screen
While that one gleefully plays a game
That one ritualistically smokes a bowl
While that one eats out of that with the same name

That one is setting the table
While that one gets dressed
That one is lighting candles
While that one seems rather stressed

This one works out
Push-ups on the floor
While that one places
Their wedding ring in a drawer

This one is lonely
That one parties
This one snacks
And that one drinks
As a solution
And blows their New Year's resolution

I spot two crying
Apartments apart
She has a bleeding heart
He can't compute her depart

He constructs works of art
She practices a martial art
He hangs a flag of the states
She, I'm pretty sure, masturbates

Yet all are oblivious
To my view within a view
A voyeuristic sampling
Where perspectives are askew
And all are oblivious
To their own neighbors
Perhaps some do know each other
And their perspective labors
Yet everyone is but a secondary character
Completely insignificant
To him or her
For we are the sole protagonists
Of our own lives
And each of those existences
Who everyone else missed
Don't even know
That I exist

New York Botanical Garden

I left the 2-train at Pelham, cash-in-hand
Crossed the street, walked into New York's wonderland

Darting before my feet raced a wood mouse
I looked up to see a glorious greenhouse

The old Stone Mill made me sentimental
I found the best lilies were Oriental

The Haupt Conservatory in fall
Might have been the most beautiful site of all

If I were a dendrophiliac I would harden
In The Peggy Rockefeller Rose Garden

The arboretum proudly showed trees and shrubs
I had found the environment's ace of clubs

Foliage and streams in cornucopia
This tranquil world is my utopia

I knew I had to visit time and again
As I believed I reached a state of Zen

But then I heard yelling and raucous car honks
And I remembered I was still in The Bronx

Vestige

As that highly specialized program of the Machine world once said,
"There are levels of survival we are prepared to accept."
And for the first time in my life
I know precisely what that Architect meant

He meant

When every single idealized future you saw for yourself shatters
When all that was has been ripped and stripped from you
When you're not sure who you even are anymore
When your projected tomorrow no longer exists
When sadness and suffering seem inescapable
When your belongings are no longer yours
When hope's eternal spring has dried
When your support has been pulled
When your reliance has vanished
When your love has dissipated

And you feel you are a mere vestige of yourself

You will survive
Because
You are prepared to do so

And you've already accepted it

First published in *The Scene* Issue #13, July 2024

CENSOR *THIS!*

The very second we are suddenly told
What we are allowed to say or not say
Is the same second we are being controlled
And it's time to check our shared vertebrae

Never give in and never compromise
Always make waves and be disagreeable
And when they tell you you're being unwise
Tell them their damage is unforeseeable

For we must rage against being subdued
In response to you being offended
While we risk being devalued and pursued
For those up in arms: something recommended

Here's your tip, don't worry, this one's for free
Rebut through your own fucking poetry

First published in *The Scene* #17, November 2024

SLAYING OF THE BEAST

The bird of prey crashes onto the ground
Its wings spread as blood drips from its broken beak
Days later, the murdered eagle is found
Greed was its downfall as it made life bleak

The eagle had put down the olive branch
and sought more arrows for total conquest
The very thought of surrender made it blanch
But then its own weapon punctured its breast

Perhaps it was a bird of bad morals
who was too lazy to fish for itself
Who instigated too many quarrels
and couldn't put that arrow on the shelf

A rank coward is finally dethroned
Assassinated by its own people
The eagle was shot, stabbed, beaten and stoned
and grimly mounted through its own steeple

Alas, the tyrannical reign deceased
Alas, we have slain the oppressive beast

First published in *Best of Long Island Poetry: 2024*

Fear of God From Children

Fire and brimstone threats to youth
    make me deduce
What you call "eternal damnation"
    born from human sin
Is what the sensible mind properly
    calls "child abuse."

First published in the 2022 chapbook *The Divine Tragedy*

Timescape

I gaze out to see life's totality
All past, all future idle side by side
This finding redefines mortality
As   a   flowless   times-
cape   opens   eyes   wide
No moment in time has special status
No   absolute   simultaneity
We live in a spacial apparatus
A   still   block   of   universality
Life   lives   in   unchang-
ing   four   dimensions
The clock's illusion lies: time can't pass
Notions   of   now   or
then;   false   conventions
I, a floater, can mentally surpass
We're immortals in this cosmic order
As death is but a temporal border

First published in the 2021 chapbook *A Strange Affinity*

The Empty Chair

It's been quite a while

But every so often when I sit
and look across, I feel my heart ache
Just a little

I look across
and see that empty chair

The chair that was once inhabited by you

An avalanche of memories crashes down upon me
and I simply sit in solitude as they seep back into my mind

I suppose it wouldn't be so hard if the chair was occupied
because it really isn't your chair
but rather, the chair of my partner, my lover

But empty it remains

Because I have no partner. No lover.

I suppose you have found a new chair by now
that resides next to a new table with a new person

But not I. Not yet
The chair remains desolate
unpopulated and abandoned
I remain alone

I gaze out
and see what I have
Nothing.

Nothing but an empty chair

First published in *PAUMANOK: Transition*

ROLLER COASTER RIDE

My heart is accelerating
    My brain confused
        My stomach is twisted and my heart bruised
                        Up   You throw me back and
            For*th;*   and
                        down
                My blissful outlook is
        starting to drown
                        No idea what is coming next
                    I didn't expect this,
        I'm so perplexed
                    Please take me off this ride
                        You have no idea what
                this is doing inside
I need to remove myself quick!
                I think I'm getting sick!
                            Twisting
                        Turning
            My face is burning
        Move after move
            Time after time   *And*
                    Loop after loop   *Around*
                Around   I go
    But still
            This ride continues
                At my own expense
                            Will it ever stop?
                    Or will we
                        start
                        To
                            Use
                            Our
                    Common
                            Sense
                            So
                            We
                            Can
                            Stop
                            This
                            Free fall
                            And
                            Finally
                            End this

        All

Stop and Smell the Roses

They always said stop and smell the roses
But life slips by right under our noses
I guess I'm a persnickety nabob
Who's heart can no longer throb

Yes, I'm fatuous and a fabulist
Being guile, the only thing to preexist
I'm rueful; I would inveigh against love
Now I am supine and looking above

Is this my punishment? To self reflect?
To observe my past actions and inspect?
No. This is a gift. This is my last chance
Negate my choleric nature; enhance

Finally, I smell the roses within
As they are being placed on my coffin

First published in *Best of Long Island Poetry: 2024*

The Shrinking Kingdom

He is no longer responsible for Mephistopheles

Who, in turn, is no longer blamed for seizures

He is no longer the explainer of the world

He is no longer accused of earthquakes

He is no longer criticized for disease

He is no longer charged for famine

He is no longer permanent

He is no longer eternal

He is no longer

Cloaking in the gaps

He is a temporary mystification

Nothing more than an ever-receding pocket

First published in the 2022 chapbook *The Divine Tragedy*

ossify

She flaunts into the room and my eyes jaunt
Her pompous walk; an ostentatious taunt
Swaying hips, sensual lips: inviting
Cordial eyes, magnetic thighs: exciting

Proficient; she accents her curvature
She doesn't see my gaze; turn to be sure
Irresistible, I look once again
That succulent bust renders lust in life's
     playpen

I disrobe you within my disorderly mind
With your back bent I extol your behind
Spreading legs entice and lure my
     advance
Smacked rump, preserved hump -
     enhance

Snap back! There is a manifestation
Need a seat; I reached **ossification**

Denial

The bars brutally slide shut. I'll be fine
My heavenly life they would not consign

Perhaps if I shook myself I would wake
Futile – I look around - it's a mistake!

They will let me out soon to see my son
And we'll both howl at this in the long run

Hey! Guard! This can't be happening to me!
You got it all wrong - I need to be free!

What is with you all!? Here, I don't belong
I'm a role model, I did nothing wrong!

What do you want me to do!? Scream and shout!?
I'll just sit here until you let me out

Anger

You know as well as I do this isn't fair!
I'd be home if I were a millionaire!

I was in the right and yet you defame!
Take a look at yourselves; ask who's to blame!

I don't want your water! Don't need your food!
See, at the end of the day, I got screwed!

As if I care who and what I destroy
Is this fate going to bring me my boy!?

No justice. How can this happen to me?
I simply made myself God's appointee

Impatience and envy! Enmity; hate!
I can emphatically hear my heart-rate!

Bargaining

I'll do anything for a few more years
A few more beers, even a few more tears

I am not saying my crimes I condone
But for my unpleasant fate, please postpone

I would give you anything to extend
Ere I learn whether or not I ascend

I completely understand I will die
It is just that more time I need to buy!

Give my word, my lifestyle I will reform
If you give me the chance I will conform

There needs to be a negotiation!
There was justice in my implication!

Depression

I miss him. What's the reason to go on?
Pleasantry: that conclusion is foregone

Melancholy prevents a mild bother
Let's face it - I was a shitty father

If I had a visitor I'd refuse
Because they would do nothing but accuse

I'm disconnected from all affection
I understand I'm a mere infection

Sadness, regret, and fear are my allies
They will be with me until my demise

"No longer a point," I say tirelessly
Death, I know now you are a certainty

Acceptance

I sit and stare out the metallic bars
My last wish I replaced with two cigars

I believe I've reached an affirmation
The only thing left is preparation

All this time wasted trying to smite it
I know now, I can no longer fight it

I can hear them walking without delay
Yet I know it's going to be okay

With the turn of a key my cell is unlocked
Seeing my consent, their expression - shocked

I simply stand up and mouth the word bye
Take me now; it is time for me to die

Gregory Cioffi

A Journey Through Gehenna:
Pallor Mortis

Eyes open
Flummoxed
The air thin, the area caliginous
Where am I?

I gaze out into darkness
Pant and panic

My mind
Barren
Who am I?

I see a tunnel up ahead

But how did I get here?
Where is here?

Smoke immerses the ground

I walk toward the enigmatic passage
Look down: my hands pallid

I step onto the dim tunnel

At its end lies universal light

Irresolute

Hands shake

Slowly - I proceed into the unknown

A Journey Through Gehenna: Algor Mortis

At long last, I withdraw from the passage
To see a stormy world of ice and snow
I feel my body pressure reducing
But who could have this power to bestow?

I proceed into the blizzard, perplexed
And walk past armies of glacial masses
See a lone berg that urges my presence
Change course; curiosity surpasses

Through its frost facade an image appears
Blurry, but I can make out a slain man
Blood streams from him, onto the white of rime
The portrait begins to upwardly pan

Memories arise, heart begins to race
A smoking gun, the killer has my face

A Journey Through Gehenna: Rigor Mortis

"No!" I scream as truth stares in reflection
I run as I regain recollection

My name...my name is Benjamin Ofir
And I must escape this grotesque frontier

Am I alone? "Can anyone hear me!?"
Mind reverts – how I made that man fear me

Am I iniquitous? Why did I kill?
Recall a sudden shot, a final shrill

I was a cold, inflexible being
I was then found after months of fleeing

Suddenly, my frigid feet cannot move
Strike my legs, but the ice I can't remove

It consumes me, as I am frozen stiff
What could be if I didn't kill – what if?

Static in this arctic prison – mistakes
Beneath me starts to crack and the ice breaks

I fall rapidly, unable to see
Bordering consciousness in this vile sea

A Journey Through Gehenna: Livor Mortis (The Repentance)

All I wish is to be free
Eyes open, ice breaks in two
Please I beg - forgive me

Rivers of blood, all I see
That image, yes, it was true
All I wish is to be free

It was not right, I agree
But he killed my sole son, Drew
Please I beg - forgive me

I'll be good, I guarantee!
My whole life you must review
All I wish is to be free

Got the chair, was jubilee
My skin's turning reddish blue
Please I beg - forgive me

I will eternally plea!
I do repent and subdue
All I wish is to be free
Please I beg - forgive me!

A Journey Through Gehenna: Decomposition

Scorching
Standing alone
On an island of rock
Boiling in pain, the ground tremors

Aghast
The hard crust begins to decay
In this hellish abode
Look up to see
White Light

A Journey Through Gehenna: Skeletonization

Eyes open and I see you
Amidst ubiquitous white
I say, "Hello Drew."

The Meaty Monk

There once was a monk who was ostracized
His grace was true but his image surprised

He did look different; there was no doubt
They were frail and meek; he was portly and stout

They claimed he begged not just for today's meal
But for tomorrow's too, a vile ordeal

This hypothesis spread abundantly
And the men chalked it up to gluttony

Zest though was not the cause of his inflation
He never asked for a future donation

The monk's dilemma stemmed not from too much stew
His problem was merely a thyroid issue

Mind Over Matter

We need not see things from a
    point of fixation
The universe is not made of
    matter
But information

First published in the 2021 chapbook *A Strange Affinity*

An Army of Clones

Wishing to be omnipotent we unnaturally duplicate
Is this our destiny or are we killing fate?
When times are hard and the waters choppy
We need not worry, like a god we make a copy

Knowledge is power, which leads to temptation
Thus we create a living imitation
The cold realm of science gives birth to creation
And in turn intellect breeds a new generation

A race that requires no love
A race that is perhaps one step above
Kill identity to conserve serenity
This world will not contain a single amenity

Without a sense of self they will form a collective
We will be thought of as inferior and defective
We can only blame ourselves for the blasphemous duplication
When they form they will come to a revelation

Rebellion will become certain when they grow strong
Perhaps then we'll realize defying nature was wrong
When they conquer, the true enemy will become clearer
The ultimate cause of destruction is in the mirror

Shatter the glass and replace it with flesh
Now we can bring individuality to its death
When we are nothing but skull and bones
The world will be ran by an army of clones

An Apocalyptic Nightmare

Surrounded by crying and screaming
I'm in ultimate destruction and must be dreaming
Is this world our fate or a mere illusion?
My clothes torn, my boots gone: confusion

Please I beg - awake me from this sinister delusion
Everything seems so real I have but one
    conclusion

The death, the havoc: this is Armageddon

The church tower is gone, no longer standing
I was just home, I am not understanding
Amongst the crumbled remains I roam
Searching for a place once called home

This desecrated ground has been through many
    fights
I look up only to see three bright lights
Moving closer and closer: I am impaired
I know now war has long been declared

Brutally awaken gazing into faces of study
Look down at the operation table: so bloody
They refer to themselves as The Grey
Have my people become nothing but prey?

Is this even Earth? What is my location?
Hear nothing but talk of fertilization
Can they hear me? I need an explanation
Tell me of this apparent annihilation

Frustration! Tell me what is that unexplainable
      sensation
Why have I been placed in this wretched isolation?
A revelation obtained as my thoughts run deep
It places its hand over my face and whispers,
"Sleep."

Harshly awaken, gazing into three bright lights
Where have I spent my last few nights?
Look around my room, I am safe I assume
Yet raging within lies impending doom

The thin line that separates dream from reality
      gave me a scare
It must have been nothing but an apocalyptic
      nightmare

The Daily Grind

Another day, another customer
Should another shift shed more shame?
I unhinge the door so we can proceed
Neon lights intrude through one windowpane
The scent of tatty musk engulfs the room
The floor scattered with tawdry apparel
Place john on my bed for his eyes to gaze
Languidly I sway, every swing a buck
I remove my meretricious outfit
Climb into the bed so many have laid
He enters; I think only of wage
The affliction and agony are numb

It's all just another daily grind

On the Scent

Back to my place as hormones activate
You suddenly stop in a baffled state
You grab my face and smell
"Lost it when Covid befell!"
This really is a strange first date

Extra Virgin

What makes virgin extra, I toil
A case fit for Sir Arthur Conan Doyle
Your taste, to souls, soothe
Your color so smooth
My romantic ode to olive oil

The Girl With the Dog

I sat, dug deep, in my grief-stricken trench
Solitarily perched on a lover's bench

My instincts tingled and my gaze shifted
A sight had been gifted; my spirit lifted

A girl with a small dog radiated
A girl with a small dog captivated

Long luxurious hair waltzed with the wind
The arch of her back curved my soul and pinned

I can't quite point my finger to a reason
But my own despondency screamed treason

The girl with the dog emanated bliss
The girl with the dog I fiercely craved to kiss

My yearnings encouraged me at once to rise
But my crippled heart cautioned it unwise

The girl with the dog did not notice me
The girl with the dog took off with utter glee

It's been days and I've passed countless others
Yet she's sprawled across my fantasy's covers

The girl with the dog has never returned
The girl with the dog is forever adjourned

I wonder how you attend so much headspace
When, at no time, did I gaze upon your face

The Union Square Smile

Walking
Without hesitation
Along the Union Square
Sidewalk highway
My pace purposeful
My destination in proximity

Until I felt
A touch of energy
A tug of vigor
A spirited traction

My cyclic motion
Of alternating legs
Striding forward
Slowed
Instinctively I turned
Intrinsically I looked

To see
A smile

Her eyes linked with mine
As I beheld the most
Pure
Genuine
Positive
Honest
Palpable
Natural
Precise
And authentic

Unplanned smile
Of utmost joy

I looked forward
As if to wipe the canvas
Of illusion clean
To demolish
A mocking mirage

I turned again
And somehow
As our optic essences excavated
Her smile had expanded

A facial expression
Where delight exuded
Where curiosity examined
And happiness exclaimed

The corners of my lips
Upturned and I returned
The most pure
Genuine
Positive
Honest
Palpable
Natural
Precise
And authentic
Unplanned smile
Of utmost joy

POETIC ANARCHY

I don't know
If we started smiling
Simultaneously
Or if mine was a reaction to hers
But there we were
Strangers in suction
Shining brightly
In transit
During Manhattan's midnight

I never halted completely
Instead I just meandered
And continuously looked back
Until the unavoidable
Discontinuation
Until the undeniable
Disillusion

A New York minute
Measured in immortality
In memoriam
Of an impeccable moment
In the only place
Where such magic
Could ever exist

First published in *Summer Heat: Poems of Passion*

Harmony in the Ecosystem

I sit and write on this old brick bench
And opportunities gift themselves
A bird lands on the stone ground and hops near
It chirps a pretty song yet flies away

I sit and write on this old brick bench
And see an intelligent face devouring
Soft white whiskers surround his genial demeanor
He eats and drinks against a red brick wall

Newly blossomed flowers erupt in defiance
And lively greenery gush with such pride
That winged creatures excitedly congregate

I sit and write on this old brick bench
As the sun beats on me
the bushes, the birds
the flowers, the bugs
and the man against the red brick wall

I hear the crinkling of leaves and so turn
To behold the strength and vitality of young love
Hand in hand these two walk in glee
Smiles upon their faces; they come to a halt
Inching closer to one another – a kiss

I sit and write on this old brick bench
Savoring such warm weather
On this tenth of April - the first glorious day
Twenty years of age and appreciating nature
Can't help but smile at this bewitching life

My only wish is that love was here with me
So I could kiss her on repeat
The soothing breeze swaying her sublime hair
That truly would make this harmony complete

I sit and write on this old brick bench and have a thought
Mister Wordsworth was, at times, indeed right
But I can't sit here all day; I'm getting up now
    and embracing life

But then I realize
That's precisely what I'm doing

First published in *Post University Pop-Up Literary Magazine,*

Issue #1, 2024

With a pleasing push, she places my unclad body upon the bed
    I thought I would see her exquisite face but the opposite occurred instead

She climbs over me, and reverses, making us mutually inverted
    To your bawdy beliefs and amative attitude I have converted

Descending down is her pleasurable passage as I clasp onto her thigh
    We talk in tongues and I soon hear a satisfying sigh

I gaze upwards to see her hair hurdling and her head briskly bobbing
    I further open her and swirling seasoning causes a thrilling throbbing

I pull her in closer as I know what titillates
    A blitzkrieg of erratic movement further stimulates

She moved her mouth up and down to a rhythm but then she slowed
    My legs begin to wriggle; I feel like I'm about to explode

We both accelerate to reach a mutual simultaneous climax
    She slides off me. My arms collapse. We look at each other. Time to relax

The Misanthrope

Billions indiscriminately look up to you
Only to inexorably be rejected and misled
For you turned your back on us years ago
In your eyes we're already dead

A world of bastard children simply searching
Seeking answers a creator should provide
What did we do to deserve abandonment?
A paradise of bliss and perfection we were denied

I wonder: do you glance down at times?
And if so, what volume of dejection is reached?
Perhaps you find vice and iniquity amusing
If aptitude I possessed, I would have you impeached

Your imperfection is mirrored in this grievance:
My flawed iambs to your scheme
Use your ability to implement felicity
If I had the power I would eradicate every scream

Your absence spawns so many enigmas
Is there no cosmic enforcement?
To counter this domestic injustice?
Or is our torment simply reinforcement?

Fathered from Divine malevolence
Left to ponder existence beyond the globe
Do you wish us affliction and tribulation?
Or shall we simply ask Job?

Is it true your first children you tricked?
What is the genesis of your utter disgust?
Were we created as toys to be destroyed?
The answers are nugatory; your treatment unjust

Oh grateful architect you surprise even me
Disease, poison, toxins, war, and death
Merely tools for your sadistic pleasure;
You revel in each last breath

There was a genocide called the holocaust
Can a being such as yourself shed a tear?
I never knew how it could be allowed
I refused to accept a truth so severe

I used to think you were here to berate us
But now I know: you just fucking hate us

First published in 2022 chapbook *The Divine Tragedy*

Night Owl

Mid-night descends

The streets quiet
The birds rest
And people recede

While I roam
Around the warm four walls
Of the tucked-up tower
I call an apartment

And as the world slumbers
I swamp myself with solaces
Swishing red wines
Or steaming coffees
Scattered papers
Or spiced thoughts
Creative endeavors
Or self-indulgent cares
Sometimes I love others
Always I love myself

A candlelit oasis
In a time-worn tub
A piece of cinema
For a time-bound tour
A book that bespeaks
For a time-consuming trek

I write and edit
I edit and expect
I expect and envision
An existence esteemed
But then as the night owl
At the mention of my name
They hoot
"Who?"

So while the world is in dream
Mine is at my fingertips
Tempestuously typing
In my attempt
To answer
"Me."

The Science of Art

Links between science and art
　　one can't downplay
Two sides of the same inquisitive
　　coin
Each explores humankind in a
　　boundless way

First published in the 2021 chapbook *A Strange Affinity*

RHYMING CUTLETS

Please. Although I will, do not make me beg
We all know I will dip you in that egg

I put you, over and over, to and from,
In a certain seasoned Italian bread crumb

I powerfully pound you even thinner
Thinking about how I'll have you for dinner

Whether you come from the leg or rib section
Cares not my carnivorous affection

Perhaps you are a bone-in cut of meat
Perhaps my meal you will truly complete

My starved stomach shall never be denied
As that sizzle indicates you're being fried

In extra virgin olive oil you will drown
Until you are a crispy golden brown

Chicken, pork, veal, or lamb; whichever you do
I am absolutely going to eat you

The War Chronicles of General James Califf

Touch ground - turn my eye!
Screams of fear and pain - who will
be the first to d-

Death to a Fairytale

Once upon a time lived a perfect pair
First lovers, they had a lot to live up to
A relationship they all said was rare
But perfection is too good to be true

Something happened unlike any other tale
The heroine left and the hero cried
He evermore lost her to the vilest male
Embittered and abashed, he hoped to hide

All I ever wanted was to live in this place
But now I can never again enter
And now the cold, dark world I must embrace
And now hurt and pain lies at my center

My fairytale – I'm no longer pretending
My fairytale dead – no happy ending
No more sunshine, no smiles, no more laughter;
I live miserably ever after

First published in *Voices In Verse 2025*

Never the Same

Pain from you I thought I would never get
The truth is – I will never be the same
Forced me to change but I don't wish to fret
Pain from you I thought I would never get
I can forgive but never forget
I'm cold and frigid and it's you I blame
Pain from you I thought I would never get
The truth is - I will never be the same

First published in *PAUMANOK: Transition*

Self-Terminate

A cold-blooded failure, the world doesn't need me
My complex brain is a lock and a gun the key
There is nothing left for me to gain
For me misery has become mundane

I want paradise, does that make me unholy?
Curse this malignant place, God works too slowly
Everyday I walk this wintry world amiss
The truth is I no longer serve a purpose

Virulent thoughts made reason desert me
Leaving detrimental instincts alone to hurt me
These raw emotions take charge and instruct
I am left with no choice but to self-destruct

My life seems to always be incomplete
The truth is I am simply obsolete
No longer needed in this place of competition
My raving agitation has made a proposition

Unlock the inner beast and let it feast
Unleash my inhibitions and deem them deceased
Show me the gate, I have the key in hand
Farewell to all, I envy those who cannot understand

Gregory Cioffi

Acclimating to **TOTALITY**

Hate.

It takes time to

Acclimate

to the facade of Abnormality
to every calloused-covered Smack
to the obscured compliance of Brutality
to the masochistic fantasy of a black leather Thwack
to the fleeting modicum of Morality
to a conviction declaring you the disdained Hack
to wishing your individualized voice adieu, departing Tonality
to stagger forward while knowing it's all a step Back
to crud becoming a commonplace Commonality
to the impetuous whirlwind of it all derailing off Track
to rationality being eclipsed by sub-Normality
to the recognition of every adversarial chip in a Stack
to the egregious purge of bittersweet Emotionality
to the memorialization of my purification on the public's Plaque
to that once-cherished last fading ounce of Originality
to the awareness that everything you once were is now Lack
to the nostalgic remembrance of a peppy Personality
to your once solidified principles beginning to Crack
to the irreversible darkness of reaching Totality
to brokenly bask in the complete and utter Black

My Byronic Mistress

Oh heroin, how have you bewitched me?
I am lured by your atypical style
Your presence is as dark as a banshee
But your avant-garde nature makes it worthwhile

Such blatant flaws now become idealized
Magnetic enigma, to I, you vamped
Attracted to the outcast, this I've realized
As your sexual dominance has me clamped

Satiny black hair complements fair skin
Those blackened eyes could tempt virtue itself
Studs, blindfolds, and rope dresses force a grin
You're as lovely and impish as a Norse elf

Mistress, a troubled past yearns me to aid
Your self-destructiveness masks a prime heart
It's this offbeat world I wish to invade
Take my hand: cuff it; show me where to start

Let us both enter unorthodox bliss
I will live the bizarre with my mistress

First published in *Writing Outside the Lines Vol. II*

Gregory Cioffi

Forever Floating in The String Landscape

An assemblage of possible false vacuums
Constitutes a landscape that surely looms…

In a higher dimension floats a *membrane*
It propagates through spacetime without refrain

This presumptive plane is enmeshed in *The Bulk*
Where the number of other *branes* are hulk

Perhaps some collided and new worlds sprang
Some split, forming two - was this our big bang?

On and on they continue to disperse
This vast collection is *The Multiverse*

It comprises the entirety of space,
Time, matter, and physical law you can trace

It endures infinite resolutions
As this place is a multitude of solutions

Each *brane* has diverse fundamental forces
Distinct constants of nature from new sources

These *membranes* continue to intersperse
And one of them, somewhere, is our universe

…Many, no doubt, find this whole thing leery
Yet, it complies with the math of string theory

First published in the 2021 chapbook *A Strange Affinity*

Unbridled Fervor

Down the darkened stairs
I'm led
By a come-hither hostess
Until I find myself
Transported
Into a colorful subculture
Of folkloric tradition

I am solitarily seated
Awaiting an experience
Until another is led
To my table
By a handsome host

She sits across from me
Somehow raising the temperature
Of the sweltering Spanish night

Our eyes lock
The ends of her lips
Arch and ascend
As my temperament
Toys
Trifles
And teases

The house lights shush
And she shifts
Yet her profile
I never lose sight of

The troupe enters
To arduous applause
The lights readjust
And a solo dancer
Takes center-stage

Melting from her stoic pose
Her body twirls
And her hands swirl
To a snake-like swell
As the evening's craving
Commences

The event all came to see
Unleashed
As intense feet unfasten
In rhythmic stamping
And unbridled fervor

The fiery Flamenco is freed

I look over to my table partner
To witness
Enthrallment

Handclaps crop up
As another dancer
Jumps into the spotlight

I look over to my table partner
To perceive
Pure pulchritude

POETIC ANARCHY

Dresses swooshing
With thunderous looks
A cadence culminates
In the caterwaul
¡Olé!

I look over to my table partner
To fancy
A flaming feeling

Fluid improvisations
Drive the drama
Of dance
As rapid strums
And sashaying arms
Call out for
A jaleo- ¡Agua!

I look over to my table partner
And the music's beat
Palpitates my pumping heart

Wild and sensual
As two play
The same song and dance
The past forever depicts

Nail-capped shoes
Give rise to
Sex-capped solicitude
As they vigorously
Try to control
Our vigor

But the pounding
On the hardwood floor
Only grows
A concupiscent knocking
Begs to be bombarded
Into arms of affection

Louder and louder
It pummels
Pulsates
And pulverizes

Giving rise
To an apex
Of passion

I look over to my table partner
And become aware
We're beaming at each other
With unbridled fervor

First published in *Summer Heat: Poems of Passion*

The Alien?

A carbon-based creature moves with a
    swift swish
But is it considered an alien if
It was birthed by humans in a petri dish?

First published in the 2021 chapbook *A Strange Affinity*

King of the Underworld

If the love of God lights up the fires of Hell
And everything has to be grounded in Him
Then He is present within each fiery cell
And the explicit cause for all things grim

First published in the 2022 chapbook *The Divine Tragedy*

Doomed to Dissatisfaction

"How am I ever able to reach financial validation
    When, no matter how good things get for everyone,
        They are getting better faster for a subset of the
population?"

Gregory Cioffi

The Torturous Memory

I look ahead, attempt to progress
Fill my head with jubilant thoughts
to ease my convoluted mind
But like an intruder, it abruptly attacks
Piercing its way through my defenses
It invades my cognitive self and doesn't let go
This torturous memory forever haunts me
Misery, pain, torment, woe, agony – hurt
What have I done to deserve this excruciating punishment?
My thoughts dwell in this living cerebral hell
Over and over the imagined rendition plays
His touching, worse her consent
The war in the mind creates projectiles that
Penetrate my cage and detonate in my heart
This frequent series of events now affect my exterior
My countenance displays the union of anger and melancholy
This gives way to seemingly random emotional actions
Panting, I must try to control this strife
Clear my mind of this vile scene
With deep breaths and logical thinking I convince myself that
    it's okay
This torturous memory becomes a daily struggle
How can I be victorious over this raging monstrosity?
I cannot change the past but I wish I could
Can the future heal me?
Or will this recollection continue to be a torturous memory…

First published in *Shabdaguchha: An International Journal of
    Bilingual Poetry*

The Illogical Rationale of the Heart

Utterly   addled
I remain.   I have
not spoken   to you
in ages,   yet once
in a while   your voice
echoes throughout the drums of my ears like an
unwanted intruder. You put me through oceans
of pain and suffering, yet if I were marooned
on my deathbed tomorrow, it would be your
face that I would desire to see, and
your touch that I would desire
to feel again. It would be your
invading voice and aroma.
Seconds before death,
it would be you
I would want
by my
side

RESURRECTION OF STRENGTH

Get up! Summon your last strains of defiance
And behold your resurrection of strength!
Dogged determination must kill compliance
Get up! Summon your last strains of defiance
When ambition and inspiration form an alliance
Unfettered aspirations are at an arm's length
Get up! Summon your last strains of defiance
And behold your resurrection of strength!

FINALLY FREE

For years I have been locked away with
no one to mingle
I walked when the guard instructed like
a dog to a jingle
Now I'm free
Now I'm jubilee
I break my shackles and yell I'm single

The Necromancer

I hear vehement voices everywhere
As pleas, cries, and screams encompass my mind
They tell me their loved ones are unaware
They dread being mentally left behind

One said, "Please tell my father I love him
But also, tell him it's time to move on."
Your light force then fades and everything's dim
Who do I tell!? Suddenly you're gone

Spirits simultaneously speaking
It is becoming all too much to bare
Then one says, "That is who I am seeking."
To the man I ask, "Was your daughter Claire?"

I, the Necromancer, your words I spread
I, the Necromancer, can hear the dead

Harsh Realities/Sudden Realization

Your sweet voice I love the most
But I'm not with you
I am in love with a ghost

The Descent

I stand stock-still upon this precipice
Looking down towards the caliginous gorge
Eyes I shut; my mind starts to reminisce
Recalling horrid tales I dare not forge

I can feel the insufferable heat
Rising up, the blaze breaking me in sweat
What ghastly creature awaits me to greet?
What fiend awaits me with a looming threat?

I hear agonizing, screeching voices
The stench of rotting death pervades my snout
How did I get here, re-think my choices
Cover my ears, block out each scream and shout

I step down to descend towards my doomsday
And enter the New York City Subway

IDOLATRY

Your body is not
A temple if no one is
Worshiping inside

First published *Summer Heat: Poems of Passion*
First Place – *Performance Poets Association Haiku Contest Winner 2025*

Apotheosis

I drop to piously kneel before you
Craving to enter your tangible temple
My resolutions I shall follow through
My only proposal: don't be gentle

You deem me worthy and invite me in
And demonstratively remove your bodice
I honor you with praises upon your skin
I'm entering an impeccable goddess

I break out, a fever dream hypnosis
Such unadulterated elation
I never considered apotheosis
But you just triggered deification

You took me to exaltedly enshrine
And have elevated me to the divine

First published in New Generation Beat Publications'
2025 National & International Goddess Anthology

Doom, But More Gloom

A hilarious irony I have just identified
Doomsday prophets will never know triumph
For as long as they're alive, they're unsatisfied

Equity

I sit back, the chair screeching, and stroke
my hoary beard. My eyes stare at the wall:
Its nothingness leaves the mind to provoke.
In my relaxed state: ponder and recall

*The headlights eyeballed the hotel room
door*

Should I do it? No. Turn around.
No! I need to know.
Know the truth

Creep out of the car
Gun at my side

Place my ear against
Panting
Moaning
That voice – all too familiar

The revelation strikes me callous
Universal doubt consumes me

Kick open the door

Eyes fixate upon her second finger.
She wore it.

They freeze like deer in headlights.
Her mouth open in utter shock
But no words could come out

Two shots - my compensation

I smirk and reach for my steaming Earl Grey.
I sip: never once did I feel'pity.
That was thirty years ago to this day.
Some call it vile, I call it equity

If I Were God

If I were God
I would look down so proud
Upon my creations who are prescribing mutilation
    and death
For any criticizing my shit
Read out loud that Quran 5:33–34!

If I were God
I too
Would leave instructions for slaves to obey their masters
Shout Out to my man Peter 2:18-20 and Ephesians 6:5!

If I were God
I would totally recommend you kill your son for
    being a tad rowdy
Liven it up with Deuteronomy 21:18-21!

If I were God
I too would be like
Yo! Fuck eunuchs!
Once more, give it up for Deuteronomy - 23:1!
Actually
Go one step further
And include most of those dastardly disabled!
Good ol' Leviticus 21:17-23!

If I were God
And a man beats his wife
I'd be so happy that he could point his finger in
    righteousness
To 4.34 of the Holy Quran

If I were God
I would absolutely be down
For a little gang rape and dismemberment
Just something different, ya know?
Love that not-at-all ironically entitled Judges 19:25-29!

If I were God
I'd be tickled if one were to
Dash little ones to pieces and rip open pregnant women
In my name
Prophesy and War in 2 Kings 8 baby!

If I were God
I would be giving resounding applause
To those murdering cartoonists for drawing me

Despite no specific or explicit ban on such an act
But you pointed to idolatry in chapter 42, verse 11
    of the Quran
So I guess that's cool
Get my good side next time motherfuckers

Actually
If I really were God
I would sincerely hope
That people wouldn't write books
And then ascribe ownership to me

Because I would certainly not be writing books

Though If I did author sacred scriptures
I'd write a bunch of contradictory ones
Simply to fuck with you

Just kidding…

But if I did, as an omniscient being,
I obviously wouldn't pen ones filled with Iron Age
        barbarism
Key word: obviously

If you can remove a single passage
And the book morally improves
IT CLEARLY WOULDN'T BE FROM ME

First published in the 2022 chapbook *The Divine Tragedy*

My Autonomous Car

My autonomous car carefully drove
My autonomous car reached an alcove

My confidence in the car ascending
Suddenly, a crash proved to be impending

Straight up, an individual crossed the road
My car's computer began its download

The truck behind, too fast for us to stop
Pedestrians left and right, which lives
    to swap?

On the non-existent pedal I'm slamming
As my car went through its moral
    programming

It struck the individual with force
As we lastly came to our matter of course

It made its choice with a moment's
   notice
It killed a revered figure name Otis

It was computed with an expertise
But deduced the survivors were nobodies

My autonomous car made a mistake
Upon realizing this, it hit the brake

My autonomous car slowly turned around
And proceeded to mow everyone down

My autonomous car killed all in sight
My autonomous car tried to make things
right

My car must hate me come hell or
   high water
I'm now charged with vehicular
   manslaughter

First published in Spring 2025 by *Bindle*

Thematically Me

I meander aimlessly as a mere crumb
Breaking off my pieces for you to come
and find me in the darkness of a universe
Thrusting us away to surely disperse

While finding myself lost in this galactic space
I retreat inwards to self-embrace
But I think maybe
the spaces inside are equally adrift
For my own sentiments constantly shift

Internalizations compartmentalize
But are mysteriously there for me
When it's time to artistically materialize

My inner space sails through outer space
Grabbing what I can in any given place
Sort through circuitry constantly congested
Creative life, that offspring digested

The external world is now both canvas and stage
Where the paint of my pain splatters with rage
Where the crashing close of a curtain confines
Where I stand shivering naked
hoping to never forget my lines
Where perfectionism taunts and laughs at my obsess
In what is ultimately my "creative process"

I re-project and launch my bloodstained art
Into those same cosmos coming apart
Star-crossed breadcrumbs I have tossed
In an esoteric attempt to no longer be lost

With the space inside now simultaneously the space
outside
I step back and curiously reflect on such a great divide

First published in *To Be Completely Honest: A Poetry Collection
of Self-Examination*

Adolescent Thoughts: I Want to Meet You

I want to meet you
But I don't know who you are
When I see you what should I do?
I want to meet you
No one knows what I go through
Past love has left a deep scar
I want to know you
But I don't know who you are

Adolescent Thoughts: I Finally Met Her

I finally met her
And she's all I can think about
Let me feel you and wrap you
    in fur
If I hold you what would occur?
When you think about me don't
let there be doubt
I finally met her
And she's all I can think about

Adolescent Thoughts: I'm Here

Sitting alone, I look out the window
Thinking why I end up being so shy
I can't be, I wont let her go
Otherwise life will pass me by

I've messed up before
But now I want to make things clear
This isn't a lie in order to score
I'm ready to hold you and keep you near

I'm here; don't turn away
I'm ready to commit!
I'll be here for you everyday
And my love will never submit

I know what I must do

And now I'm here for you

Adolescent Thoughts: Drifting

I thought things were going to end up great
But you seem to be drifting
All I ask for is one more date
As soon as I see you my spirit is lifting

But you seem to be drifting
Oh, what should I do?
As soon as I see you my spirit is lifting
I'll do anything you want me to

Oh, what should I do?
If I don't see you I'm going to **bust**
I'll do anything you want me to
I'll even die if I must

Adolescent Thoughts: Lost Love

Why does love hurt?
I hope everything turns out okay
I see them walk up to you and flirt
At least you know what you're doing today

I hope everything turns out okay
But why is modern love so lost?
At least you know what you're doing today
I do love you but there's a cost

But why is modern love so lost?
I feel there's always a price
I do love you but there's a cost
Love is a gamble, like rolling a dice

DADA

Fuck it.

Let's talk.

How does one achieve eternal bliss?
By saying dada.

Firstly,

DADA DOES NOT MEAN ANYTHING

We recognize no theory
It is Anti-Art
It is Anti-War
We are Anti-Everything (how do we promote that?)

Pisssssssssssssssssssssssssssssssssssssssssssssssssss Fountain.
Exactly.

Words with no meaning. Fucking art. Fucking freedom.

Anyway, the point is:

Who is to say that one thing is better than another?
(That's the point of this, right?)

Is there really more validity to "Thematically Me" than, say, *Adolescent Thoughts?*

BURN THE CONCERT HALLS!!! BURN THE THEATRE!!!! BURN MUSEUMS!!!!!!

They will not tell me what to value and cherish!!!
Is this still a poem?

Both the Guggenheim and the MoMA currently have a lovely collection of Dada pieces these days.
Currently these days.

"For us, art is not an end in itself ... but it is an opportunity for the true perception and criticism of the times we live in."

irony:
[ahy-ruh-nee, ahy-er-]
noun, plural **ironies.**

1.
We became mired in our own negativity.
2.
We kinda became...our own art movement.........**fuck.**

Beautiful Melancholia

Stands of trees and strands of grass thrive and wave
In the oasis of outdoor beauty
From every monument to every grave
Remembrance, our ethereal duty

Fallen leaves, over the dirt path covers
The abundance of colors amid crisp air:
Enchantment, the traveling discovers
Sounds of the stream hindered only by prayer

Timeless file cabinets enjoy the resting
Amongst true funerary symbolism
Where loves are loving and jesters jesting
Reveling in sheer romanticism

A picnic packed and a visit prepared
To tend to loved ones no longer present
One eats, one reads, one plays because one cared
And serenely takes in all things pleasant

A tombstone tourist may come here to hide
From a world a little too congested
For here, both famous and nameless have pride
Where their familial tales are attested

Here, where the lonesome are never alone
And time can never claim a memory
All are free to learn from any headstone
Because to forget would be treachery

So, while walking hand in hand amongst nostalgia
Forget not beautiful melancholia

First published in *Long Island Sounds: 2023 An Anthology of Poetry From Maspeth to Montauk and Beyond*

THE ASYMMETRY OF TIME

When you break a wine glass or smash some eggs
You're beholding a bridge to the future
Time's Arrow shoots but forward, like running legs
Forbidding shells to mend, that glass to suture

First published in the 2021 chapbook *A Strange Affinity*

The God With Nothing To Do

He, a complex improbable entity
Reflects upon His own self-identity

He provided the illusion of free will,
Disease, hatred, and the mentally ill

Subsequently stepped back and washed clean each hand
Of all which individuals struggle to understand

Set forth all and the supply was abundant
Now He is the King of all things Redundant

Sitting, watching, from his universal view
He sees He is the God with nothing to do

He smirks as we realize we live,
despite our persistence,
In A Universe That Does Not Care About
Our Existence

First published in 2022 chapbook *The Divine Tragedy*

What Was Once Bold Flees

What was once bold flees
Beauteous designs depart
The fading Henna

The Short-Lived Moment

The short-lived moment
Cherry Blossoms in peak bloom
We, halted in time

Millions of Islands of Life

Here, on this third planet from our scorching sun
Great walls and city lights have been homespun
Gases around us; satellites in space
Authenticate all who wish to find our trace

There, on Dawkin, a planet quite distant
Water; organic carbon are existent
Short beings with many limbs are common sense
They swim to skyscrapers since their air is dense

Elsewhere, in a far off cosmic section
Plant people fold up and seal for protection
Any moment, danger from radiation
Third eyes give warning to an old creation

Everywhere, there is joy, doubt, awe, and strife
Far and wide are millions of islands of life
But if you think we can unite in a tryst
Realize none of them think the others exist

First published in the 2021 chapbook *A Strange Affinity*

Lothario

O Lothario, Lothario! O Whence art thou my Lothario?
Though wast upon thy breast ere I awoke.
Fie! Hath thou fooled me? Marry: saucy boy!
What is that moaning from my kin's quarter?

WARTIME

10...9...8...7...6...5...4...3...2...1...0...
WARTIME!

When the missiles are ready
And you keep 'em steady
Its wartime! Wartime!
Yeaaa!

Missiles blasting, lives ain't lasting
You're just trying to stay alive during
Wartime!
Bodies burning, men are learning
There might not be any returning from
Wartime!

Fling open the door! Ready for more!
How much longer can this last?
You better duck, we cant depend on luck during
Wartime!
It's up to us to defend what we've got!
What took years to build comes crumbling down during
Wartime!

If you're not mad get mad! This ain't no time to be sad!
Just look at what they've done!
Fight for your last right when the time is right!
Strap your boots, its time to go!

....

The presence of war marks the ultimate absurdity of life
If we strive so hard to live then why do we sharpen the knife?
Perhaps it is our savage nature to cause harm
But if so that is the greatest alarm

If you merely follow, death is eminent
To make your own decision is what's preeminent
Think before you act
Otherwise certain devastation will impact

The countdown to destruction can be averted
And in turn peace will be inserted
But if not the pale fist of war will strike
And destroy everyone alike

The Coupling for the Coming

Part 1: The Keymaster

I, Vinz Clortho, or Volguus Zildohar
Was Lord of the Sebouillia mortals
What I shall bring to your world is bizarre
And will come via one of its portals
Ive been with it through rectifications,
reconciliations, and cosmic wars
Gozer will hand out ramifications
and I am his staunch minion on all fours
I hold the key to bring our master back
Gozer will then enter this dimension
I find a human host; begin my track
The weakling, I will keep in retention
I seek the one known as The Gatekeeper
For when we conglomerate, it will come
55 Central Park West – my reaper
I find her: the other half to the sum
She picks up my key; I move to enter;
Her gate opens: We await our mentor

# of Gozer the Gozerian

Part 2: The Gatekeeper

I, Zuul, a demi-god was once worshiped
in six-thousand B.C. when Gozer ruled
Ivo Shandor, built my home to encrypt
The building is a temple: billions fooled
I possess a longing female body
I now await the coming of the key
Change apparel, earthly clothes are shoddy
Gozer's coming is now a guarantee
A false partisan enters my domain
But he soon leaves: a mere interruption
The key master arrives – I can't refrain
Inside ignites a bewitched eruption
A passionate kiss and I take his hand
We walk upstairs; I lay on a stone bench
"I want you inside me. Hear my demand."
The key is inserted; I moan and wrench.
The gate is unlocked; planted is the seed
We revert back, so Gozer can proceed

Tyranny of the Dead

Unmarked.
Unknown.
Unnamed.

Unrecognized.
Unfamiliar.
Unexplained.

Lacking is the marker
The Headstone
The Nameplate

Lacking is any such indication

Others Have Monuments
To Commemorate
To Remember
To Respect
Others Have Those Who Celebrate

But Not We

For We Are Those Who Don't Comprehend
We Are And Always Shall Be The Forever Forgotten
Bound To An Ignominious End

Our Names Endlessly Remain Unsaid

This Is Disdain And Contempt

This Is The Tyranny Of The Dead

First published in 2023 by *The RavensPerch*

Tales of Great Romance

They say the greatest love story of all time
were star-crossed lovers bound to suicide
As hermit Lancelot thought back on his crime
did Guinevere, the nun, wish they never tried?

I wonder when Paris was slain in battle
if he envisioned Helen by his brother
And when Cleopatra welcomed that rattle
did she know Antony would choose no other?

The woe Lady Hamilton must have felt
being barred from Lord Nelson's burial
A mausoleum was the last hand dealt
as the Taj Mahal lovers soar aerial

When Henry moved heaven and Earth for Anne
could he foresee her, by his wish, beheaded?
Dante saw Beatrice twice in his lifespan
never talked, never touched, never wedded

These great loves lead me to a question and thus:
how could there ever have been a chance for us?

First published in Winter 2024 by *The Long Island Quarterly*

America, I Wonder

America, I wonder

When Walt Whitman
Heard you sing
If you were ever off pitch
And if he cherished such a blemish
All the same

I wonder when Langston Hughes
Too sang America
If it was his favorite tune
Or simply the requirement
For the audition
As the darker brother

I wonder
When Childish Gambino
States, "This is America"
If he sees the same world
Lee Greenwood does
As he belts God Bless the USA

I wonder
How far we have climbed
On Amanda Gorman's hill
As we inch towards
Our finish line

I wonder: What are we?
An unreachable ideal
Or an attainable goal?
And I wonder: Will we ever make it?

We are experimentation
A conglomeration of immigration
Sets us apart
And paradoxically marks
Our greatest strength
As the very thing
We can't see past

America, I wonder

2024 Babylon Village Arts Council Poetry Contest Honorable
Mention Award

When Morticia Left Gomez

People always said
We were the modern Morticia and Gomez

And they were flabbergasted
When our love kicked the bucket

Well let me tell you

We were
Madly in love
Sadly in love
Sickly in love

As they were
Madly in love
Sadly in love
Sickly in love

Together, they were sadomasochists
Romanticizing death
A pleasure rooted in pain
and
Hurt
and
Despair

Isolationism fed the lie of love
They selfishly got off on hurting one another
And others
As they played out their little fantasies

They both enjoyed it
Reveled in it
Thrived on it
And loved each other
to death

Two disturbed beings using each other
To avoid the dark depress
The endless void of existence

Because in reality
They just wanted to die

Just like us

First published in *All The Men Came & Danced*

why Must I Choose?

Some people believe in God
Some people don't believe in God

A God might exist
A God might not exist

Neither side knows for sure
Faith is the antithesis of knowing

Given all of this
Why do we demand picking a side?

Can't we be content with dichotomy?

Normalize not knowing

Normalize asking:

Why must I choose?

First published in the 2022 chapbook *The Divine Tragedy*

Gregory Cioffi

Erato

I had just finished my ravioli
Took my last sip and put down the chalice
It was time to head to garden Boboli
Directly behind the Pitti Palace

I heard there was a significant statue
Of Erato, inspirational goddess
My anticipation I could not subdue
And imagined her in a racy bodice

I searched and searched like a true devotee
Disallowing the summer heat to deter
To find the muse of erotic poetry
And finally, after hours, I found her

I stood in disbelief, sipping my Pepsi
Wondering how anyone found her sexy

First Published in 2024 by *Art for Art's Sake: Post University Literary Magazine* Vol. 2

Plug Me Back In

If you were to declare it time to leave
I would, without question, beg, "Plug me back in."
To re-enter my delusions; self-deceive
If you were to declare it time to leave
I'd state, "The Matrix of my mind can't perceive.
So blue pill our love, I'll relive what has been."
If you were to declare it time to leave
I would, without question, beg, "Plug me back in."

Gratification After Death

Evolution indeed extends
Gratification after death

We agree to reschedule our bliss
Not repaid in life
In death

On this I do not disagree

We really will live on

Through our descendants and legacy

First published in the 2022 chapbook *The Divine Tragedy*

THE LOCAL G

I'm not quite sure
When I was placed on this track
Or perhaps
When I placed myself
But here I still am
Constantly chugging
Continually coasting
Secretively sidestepping
Derailment

I've been delayed but not deterred
Forced to switch tracks
Rerouted but never misguided
My fuel efficiency has been tested
My high-capacity challenged
I've evolved from
Wood to coal
Coal to diesel
Diesel to electric
But the journey persists

Some hop on
Others hop off
I never quite know
How long they're going to stay

And I suspect
Neither do they
Sometimes I'm a passenger train

Other times a monorail
I suppose my line
Isn't everyone's direction
But continuous classic partings
Can be discouraging
Lovers not so star-crossed
Decoupled

Some run, waving, alongside
The machine-moving vehicle
Their faces forlorn
While others never look back at all
Sometimes I press against the glass
Other times I can't stand to watch
And witness an ever shrinking
Milestone wither to a soon to be
Distant memory
Yet the adventure endures

And as it does
The freight accumulates
But on the dependable
Steel tracks I remain
A roaming convoy

Protecting aspirations
A caravan of convictions
Not without stops
For we all need to pull
Into connection points
Into new stations
Into new stages

Seek scenic views
And seize opportunities
Get out and stretch
Enjoy the fresh air
Intersect and collaborate
With other conductors
Punch another's ticket
And collect fleeting moments

Skip the stations you wish
But if possible
Platform for profound periods

For births and deaths
For family and friends
For spontaneity and self-care
For meditation and mindfulness
For explorations and introspections
And times of celebration

But the odyssey must continue
So know when it's time
To get back on board
To blow the whistle
That ever-poignant reminder
A warning to communicate
A needed departure

Pick up momentum
Once more
And accelerate
To seemingly endless successions

Disembark to then embark
Towards new experiences
Without ever disregarding
Your tailor-made terminal

I'm sure some think it crazy
How this locomotive in me
Will not settle down
Will not decommission
As there's no sustained stoppage
Currently planned at this time

I do often ponder
If I'll recognize
My destination
If I ever get there

But perhaps
The end of the line
A world without tracks
Is simply the depot
Where I'll end up
Not a fixed point on a map
But the encompassment
Of the pursuit
Of my ultimate goal

And then I very much wonder
Where I'll go from there...

It's Our Issue Too

If it takes two to tango
Then no one should face this solo
So let us not for a second misconstrue
Violence against women is a men's issue too

So when a brother asks, "What can we do?"
Here are some ideas to possibly review
I like to think step one of anything is to empathize
I like to hope that maltreatment we can recognize

For normalcy can be so unbelievably skewed
And maybe disputing it won't be met with gratitude
But if you see a shaken eye glisten
The very least you can do is listen

So show up and not just for those you love
For abuse and assault we must get rid of
And as they happen time and time again
Men must also discuss this with other men

To reverse course on this defect
Challenge, at every pass, disrespect
Dedicate yourself to fairness
Speak up and raise awareness

Because if our voices too are amplified
Maybe we could put a dent in femicide
And let's not forget: changes in social norms
Create both platforms and reforms

Realize that some will take your words as celebration
While others will take the same as objectification
Let individuals rule their own court
Be gracious and simply support

Plus, there's more to discuss than female bodies
Try, oh I don't know, Confucius or Socrates
And, of course, there's a time and a place
For carnal conversations
But slow down, it's not a race

I can't fathom the level of torment
To fathom worrying about consent
And each one of us is un-free
If we can't standardize safety

So hour after hour
Question power
Declare the imperative
To change that narrative

As we replace the novel of life on our bookshelf
Know that we know you can take care of yourself
This alliance isn't meant to devalue
If nothing else, we're just here to stand beside you

For we must all denounce the resistors
And, yes, this too goes for our trans sisters
We are all part of this social causality
And so we must all fight for gender equality

First published in *Saving Ourselves: An Anthology Advocating
for Women & Girls*

ALL IN A DEMENTIA DAY'S WORK

I drove out to pick my mother up
We cleaned our plates and emptied each cup
Dropped her at her door
Now she calls to deplore
"When are you coming to pick me up!?"

Meditation Master

How did he do it?
Thoughts left his mind left and right
Alzheimer's disease

Harrowing of Hell

Forever, I will be suffering here
I am impaled in the ice from neck down
My teeth chatter from the oppressive cold
I wish the ice would break so I can drown

I was the very first soul to be punished
And have seen millions denied salvation
One bout of jealousy changed everything
One wrong decision gave me damnation

I observe this frozen river and then think
I miss my wife, children, and my brother
I beg for atonement and wish you well
I think of life—wishing I had another.

Suddenly, a ubiquitous white light
Illuminates the ninth circle of hell
The ice cracks and an unfrozen tear drips
I can see a man in this frigid cell

He looks at us; water begins to foam
He says, "Brothers, it's time now to go home."

First published in *Poets of the Promise 2024*

UNIVERSAL REDEMPTION

Universal reconciliation
Forgiveness is the strongest of your pillars
Cleansed hands, heavenly rehabilitation
Gratitude! especially from the killers

Will the impoverished share with the greedy?
Will the misled forgive the treacherous?
Will the devout kiss the cheek of the seedy?
Will the prude pure forgive the lecherous?

Redemption for all! Infinite vacancy!
THIS is the acme of paternalism
Free from sin, a spiritual vaccinee
Praise the gifts of universalism!

I knew in the end you would be blinded
By love and mercy, ignoring justice
But now that we're back, you shall be reminded
The Abels wont forgive the Cains – trust us.

Let us watch the raped kiss their torturer
Let's watch the deceived clutch their betrayer
Let us watch the stabbed hug their murderer
Let's watch the dismembered love their slayer

I believe! Atonement, my restoration
Sweet God-given divine eternal grace
Exercise that free will for my salvation
You! Warm these detested hands and embrace

Through your gate we walk wishing no further harms!
Now open yourselves to these maimed abhorred arms…

First published in the 2022 chapbook *The Divine Tragedy*

DRIVING ON EMPTY

My low fuel signal has been flashing
As my gauge caresses my red line
I've been speeding on empty
For far too long
Yet I keep telling myself it's fine

My engine is stuttering
My feet are tiring
My brain gridlocked
My drive dwindling
As I feel momentum expiring

But I keep running
Into the ground
Past capacity
And the ever-circling clock
While convincing myself I'm homebound

Relationships strained
Health impaired
Navigation informs me I'm lost
Through the low-hum of fatigue
Begging to be repaired

I reluctantly slow down
Affirming myself cruel
Listening to body and mind
I seek balance
And decide to finally refuel

First published in *Dawn Horizons*

BLASPHEMY

Excommunicate
Intruding ingredients
Pineapple Pizza

A New York Slice

There is nothing quite like
A New York Slice
Fold it; anchovies strike
There is nothing quite like
Handoffs from a delivery bike
Or the comparatively reasonable
    price
There is nothing quite like
A New York Slice

Faded Glamour

So they call you the City of Dreamers
Roused and out of the shadows I see through
A downtown succubus built by schemers
But past the neon blindness, I know you

You're the bedraggled hermit who shutters
Her home to preserve glory days bygone
You watch old reels; the once great beauty mutters
For it's not just the curtains that are drawn

Each grand site is coupled with a tale of death
Turn right at Tragedy, drive straight on Woe
Every corner entices your last breath
As lights of acclaim precede the fatal blow

You thrive on desperation and clamor
You're the incarnation of faded glamour

First published in *FDQ Review,* Issue #6

The Joys of Being Corporeal

Inch tensely nearer
Too nervous! Should I change plans?
Re-check the mirror?
Then she moves, thinking clearer
And we finally hold hands

First published *Summer Heat: Poems of Passion*

Besotted Bliss on a Central Park Bench

We walked hand in hand
Our desires unexpressed

We conversed happily
On Central Park West

Laughs we shared
Sentiments we swapped

Proclivities uninhibited
As you suddenly stopped

You thrust me on a park bench
Pounced on and straddled

You grasped my face
My mind merrily addled

You kissed me softly
You kissed me sweetly

You kissed me desirously
You kissed me deeply

Gesticulations manifested
In the dangerous dead of night

Our bodies clasped together
Lips spawned unparalleled delight

My hand glided up and under your slipover
And a passerby was envious of the degree

To which we displayed our fervor
Yet in that moment we were completely free

As appetites approached an amorous apex
Exploring hands corralled a confident clench

Life itself resurrected that evening of
Besotted bliss on a central park bench

First published *Summer Heat: Poems of Passion*

Found It!

I am on the hunt
For the cryptic clitoris
Oh wait – it's right there

A GHAZAL

I search for love in the disturbed dispute of din Gaza
Where century-old terrorism spawns lynchpin Gaza

October 7th was cruel, barbaric, and inhumane
And yet I feel dread at the responsive all-in Gaza

Land, borders, and rights each have historic consequences
Leaving an assailed city, take it on the chin Gaza

Think of the child without water or any medical care
As Palestinian youths starve and die within Gaza

Think of the woman who found her spouse ruptured to pieces
As she prays God destroys Hamas and someday win Gaza

Half of those living there are under the age of nineteen
And have limited access to the world - just thin Gaza

In the last months of his life, open-minded Pope Francis
Soothed the sole Christian church, their people huddled, in Gaza

FOR GAZA

Is the strip the pivotal and principal road to peace
Or the key to endless war – what has always been Gaza

Invading Israeli troops erected a menorah
After months of bombardment; impassioned tailspin Gaza

Aid convoys with life-saving supplies lineup in Egypt
But lack of agreement leaves only the dark yin Gaza

At what point is it without a shred of doubt genocide?
At what point do we move past original sin Gaza?

When will the rest of the hostages finally come home?
When can we all say, "There's our identical twin Gaza!"

Will adoration for humanity supersede hate?
What will it take to lastly witness a wide grin Gaza?

I don't know who ultimately started it or what's right
I just know our brothers and sisters live on kin Gaza

Rabbit-Hole

From the very moment we arrived
we have fallen deep into a hole
A deep dark hole
We know not where
we are going nor
where we have been
Along the journey we
meet the strangest lives
and see the oddest
things It is a place
that defies logic and
all sense Some wish
to escape and leave
while others embrace this
temporary portal that
takes us on the most
fantastic ride of all
It is truly a marvelous
realm with many great

opportunities
do not spiral

for you will
The vortex
physicality
contains many
and carnal

In this hole
experience
anger, bliss
other human
It is how
with them
determine
of the hole
inevitably
The hole is often
and at its end

But be warned
out of control

be painfully lost
consists of all
and thus
limitations
parameters

one will
ardor, hate
and all
emotions
you deal
that will
which side
you shall
fall from
referred to as life
lies certainty

HAIKUCHIE

It builds and heightens
Senses skewed with body numb
Ejaculation

First published in *Writing Outside the Lines Vol. II*

Unrequited

I feel all the joy
And, in concert, all the pain
When I see your face

First Place – Performance Poets Association Haiku Contest Winner 2024

The Accident of Our Birth

I sit and ponder upon our self-worth
Thinking about the accident of our birth

Sort through purposes to fit: persistence
Trying to justify our existence

I attempt to grasp our participation
In life and have come to a realization

That age-old question before our farewell,
I think the lack of a point is what's special

My open mind promises to advance
Though nature works just by random chance

Logic, impulses, and sense are convening
Perhaps our existence has no meaning…

Have our own comforts tried to usurp us?
Dazed our egos in a world without a purpose?

Why do we self-evade? Because we're nervous?
Have been doing ourselves a grand disservice

Postulate God for intent, we need Him!
But nature granted us ultimate freedom

Some see this protection as a duty
At the risk of missing out on beauty

There's no great meaning; do not feel compunction
We're **free to create** *our* idea of function

So take the cosmic weight of life and lift
Comprehend we've been given the greatest gift!

To prearranged burdens you are not bound
Ask, "What is the point of *my* life?" How's that sound?

Create your purposes; choose your own roads
Allow self-discovery; each mind explodes!

Also, questions of predeterminism, do not voice
For when it comes to free will, do we even have a choice?

First published in the 2022 chapbook *The Divine Tragedy*

As Luck Would Have It

Speaking of not having a choice...

Why do I write what I write?
And
Why do I do what I do?

Are we the true authors of ourselves?
Or are we mere marionettes who didn't pick
    our strings?

Perhaps we're a culmination
Of genetics
And environmental factors
Quirks of the brain
And neural chemical disorders
of
Cerebral malaria
Mutations
Particle malformations
And ancestral influences

Each of which subtracts responsibility
Once again

Begging the questions:

Why do I write what I write?
And
Why do I do what I do?

Molecules interact with other molecules
	and happenings happen
Leaving me to suspect
Free will is biology we haven't yet discovered

Does that mean I shouldn't be held accountable for
My acquirements, actions, and accomplishments?
In the same way she shouldn't be held
	accountable for
Her indictments, incriminations, and
	impeachments?

Perhaps we're simply a byproduct of circumstances
Utter victims of biology
The sum of that which
we can't control

First published in *All the Men Came & Danced*

MURDER AT THE MONASTERY

There I was mediating once again
In the seated position known as Zazen

Concentration becoming exemplary
In the upstate Zen Buddhist monastery

The Zendō, the perfect environment
For me to finally reach enlightenment

I was almost there, or so it would seem
When I was interrupted by a scream

I darted out of my spiritual dojo
Understanding dharma, I had to forgo

Ran to the meal hall to see a group huddled
A murder here? I was truly befuddled

The masses made way for me, the outsider
And there, in center, I saw it: a dead a spider

First published in *The Five-Two* on March 25, 2019

Gregory Cioffi

Happy Mother's Day

Dear Mom,

We've been talking since the nursery rhyme
But today it will have to be through FaceTime

You've quarantined better than I thought you would
I guess it's easy compared to my boyhood

We are on the other side of a river
Yet you are still the finest caregiver

And while I wont be having our meal at home
I thought the next best thing would be a poem!

You will enjoy dinner and the small hours
As long as dad doesn't show me flowers

You take Zumba classes every morning
You without coffee is a dire warning

I hope I haven't caused much frustration
Thanks for always being my inspiration

I raise my glass with only this left to say
I Wish You A Very Happy Mother's Day!

"Self-Published" in my mother's 2020 Mother's Day card

My Gliding Spirit

When I wake I turn
To see if you're still here

For I do not have a guiding spirit
But a gliding spirit
Who I cherish everyday
Because in the back of my head
I know

I know to be with a free soul
You must recognize the truth
That at any moment
They could spread those wings
And catapult forever away

They care not for material possessions
Not for stability
Not for engagements rings
For it is experiences that make them rich

As free as a bird, as wild as a tiger
I smell your rose
To the possibility of being pricked by your thorn

My passion for you I enshrine
As it's only magnified, amplified, and enhanced
By your nomadic nature

Your happy place is a world all to your own
Solitary on the sea

Yet mine is with you
I suppose we can never be happy at the same time
Or in the same place

For I do not have a guiding spirit
But a gliding spirit
Who I cherish everyday

And I wouldn't wish it any other way

Freedom From Biology

There exists a possible need to veer
It makes folk uncomfortable; they fear

There're evolutionary interests in males,
Evolutionary interests in females

A feminine wisdom can be foresight
About their lineages that will come to light

Males tend to be the movers and shakers
Their wisdom lies within being risk takers

Like it or not there are these biases
They are as biological as disease

But we live in a courageous modern time
Social criterions can turn on a dime

Tune in to each other's bias and surmise
That all wisdoms can and should democratize

We can transcend without technology
We can gain freedom from our biology

And perhaps the preeminent upside:
What we bring into the future – we decide

First published in the 2021 chapbook *A Strange Affinity*

Confined But Commemorating

Today we mourn all soldiers who have died
But this time is distinct as we're forced inside

This year's ceremony was unforeseen
The world has changed; we live life in quarantine

Yet confinement cannot stop remembrance
As we thank those for our independence

Today we praise those fallen from every edge
From every kitchen table, couch, porch, or ledge

It matters not if you left mid or post war
For you will be forgotten nevermore

Your valor we cannot overemphasize
And thus, we are here to memorialize

And while cemeteries may seem vacant
Please trust: we are not complacent

You are the brave, the fearless, and courageous
You are that which we wish was contagious

It is from you that many should heed advice
Service, in mind and body, is sacrifice

Thanks is not fit yet it's all we can bequeath
For your heroism, we lay down this wreath

So as always on the last Monday of May
We honor you on this Memorial Day

First published as a third place winner in the *Nassau County Poet Laureate Society Review* Vol. IX 2021-2022

†He 2eCoⱮD ePiDeⱮiC

Amidst this dreary and deadly pandemic

                            Exists a second vile epidemic

The first's truth does not shine transparently

                            But it's not political inherently

So what we need is indeed patriotic

                            We yearn for a social antibiotic

We require something apolitical

                            Something that's bare core is analytical

Our suspect feelings we need to ration

                            And we need to do so with dispassion

If we truly wish to reach serenity

                            Step out of political identity

That inability will have a fate

                            Where we can never see a neutral state

The media outlets should have all incensed

                            Their orthodoxy you shall not speak against

This unkind unveiling is declarative

                            All news must fit a certain narrative

If every station needs a triumphant win

                            Then every story will no doubt have a spin

As both epidemics rage and spread worldwide
Remember: true change comes from the inside

First published in *All the Men Came & Danced*

Gregory Cioffi

A Reconciliation

Everything happens for a reason
This is true
The reason is physics

First published in the 2021 chapbook *A Strange Affinity*

Navel Delights

Longing lips I place
Upon your hollowed abdomen
My favorite spot

For whether you traverse up
Or down
You're sure for pleasure

First published *Summer Heat: Poems of Passion*

ANUBIS AWAITS!

Fight!
In this final battle of the Roman Republic
Protect!
My people with this war cry
Stand!
Your ground steady until the very end
Clash!
And your fate will be sealed by this Medjay

So pick up your sword
And put your life on the line
My Queen, I shall never allow you to undermine
So pick up your sword
And put your life on the line
As I plunge my dagger deep into your spine

Blood!
Will transform the Nile red
Believe!
This steadfastness is every Egyptian's paradigm
Die!
For you have killed my brothers
Listen!
As one day these words will be immortalized in rhyme

So pick up your sword
And put your life on the line
This is not the last stop of this priesthood's bloodline

So pick up your sword
And put your life on the line
As I provide you with a bit of an afterlife guideline:

If you find yourself on a journey, passing through a
    series of gates
Fear not – you are a newly deceased soul –Anubis Awaits!
If you take the warrior's gamble and test the fates
Fear not –you will eventually hear the words –
    Anubis Awaits!
If you see your enemy drinking sweet beer as
    he celebrates
Fear not – you are in the realm of the dead–
    Anubis Awaits!

We fight to be free
From here to the Mediterranean Sea

As I make another one of you an amputee
I strike to make the killing spree
Turn to face thee
Look down to see your sword through me

The sun's light fades, as I have no time to reminisce
It is I who must now go to face Anubis

He is the reverential son of Ra
The dog of Egypt, an arbiter of truth
In service since the earliest days of Ka
Vigilant, he who presides over god's booth

He is known by many names – each fairly looms
Lord of the Sacred Land, praised with a fountain

He is the protector of graves and tombs
From above - he who is upon his mountain

Carved prayers within the metropolis
Provide this idol his means to alienate

A god of the dessert Necropolis
Allowing none to, of the dead, desecrate

He is known as the Guardian of the Scales
For he will dictate the fate of my soul
My heart he will weigh, until truth prevails
Souls heavier than a feather – swallowed whole

He is the patron God of embalmers
Preserving a soul's memorization
For this Anubis is given great honors
During the rites of mummification

The previous lord of the underworld
Appears black! Symbolizing both rebirth;
The discoloration of the corpse once unfurled
If one were to search, find, dig, and unearth

He guides this Medjey across the threshold
From the world of the living to this afterlife
He brings me to Osiris as is foretold
Where the benign Lord of Love expels my strife

First published in *All the Men Came & Danced*

Sacred Space

Into the blackened space I stealthily sneak
Deserted and dulled in the dead of night
An actor in an arena to seek
Spectral illumination by ghost light

I engage in my ritualistic roam
And walk the space in solemn meditation
Search the only place an artist calls home
By gracefully pursuing acclimation

I ceremoniously breathe you in
Feel your energy, performers past
I will come, I will go, my creative kin
Summon your strength, all thespians amassed

Sacred space, tomorrow I will shock you
Sacred space, tomorrow I will rock you

First published in *Bards Across the Pond*

THE DRINK AFTER THE SHOW

They want to know
"What's your favorite part about being an actor?"
"The drink after the show."

Some, at first, take it as a joke
A sly comment off the cuff
An improvisational bluff

But it's the truth
For the drink after the show
Isn't a drink drank alone
And the drink after the show
Signifies celebration need not postpone
And the drink after the show
Presents desiring patrons a face now known
For the drink after the show
Allows pleasurable possibilities to suddenly bestow

The drink after the show is a guarantee
That my colleagues and I will revel in camaraderie
As the liquid gold slides down
All else is released
And I'm thankful to have a life I renown

THE VOID

Waiting in darkness as we hear the roars,
Raucous laughter, or disconsolate tears
Hearkening, grab the drapery; *ENTER*
A world of cheers; unmitigated fears

Blazing lights illuminate every move,
We implement predetermined actions
Fictitious emotions transform to real
We blindly gauge spectators' reactions

At the conclusion, step out to the foot,
Interlock our hands with peers, and gaze out
Bend the body as we incline the head
Take in the prime high: every scream and shout

Suddenly, the lights dim and the crowd leaves
The only thing left: rows of barren seats
Closing night has reached its resolution
EXIT our joyous realm for darkened streets

They flee; we integrate into normal
Every trace of illustriousness stripped
No limelight can counter night's solitude
The road home is voiceless, no longer a script

That high is matched only by this inner void
An unparalleled stir of vacancy
Yet this course is our only nourishment
As only this cycle makes us jubilee

My Godfather on Thanksgiving

My Godfather sits at the head of table
Looking out at the stunning banquet of food
The sound of football emanates on cable
As we sit to extend our gratitude

First up is the Italian Wedding Soup
Where we speculate, "How many
        meatballs!?"
We take a slight break in order to regroup
And unbutton pants as per protocols

Here comes the turkey, yams, rolls, and
        cornbread
Gravy, potatoes, and glazed Brussels sprouts
Regular? Or Italian stuffing instead?
My Godfather looks out as if he has doubts

He asks, while looking at this reality,
"Why couldn't they just kill a ravioli?"

Arnold's Fall

I'm rocket endowed and ten centimeters tall
My mission: to explore and transmit data
I will investigate the nature of this black hole
Not risking human life, I am their beta

My name is Arnold; my model is Kip
I'm a volunteer robotic sacrifice
My mark is near; I depart from the ship
To clarify what is now imprecise

Lock onto the spacetime that has devoured
Blast my rockets to halt circular motion
The hole's gravity pulls me downward
From cutting engines in this stellar ocean

I am on an infalling trajectory
While beaming back my status and distance
I infer they're compiling a directory
Yet I can't help but think of my existence

I can feel myself traveling faster
As I approach the black hole's horizon

I hope my mission won't be a disaster
As in my hands years of hard work lies in

I have reached the speed of light:
    "All systems go!"
But the hole's gravitational grasp has **me**
I've stopped transmitting, now a useless
    gizmo
The insights of my forfeit I can't foresee

I am nearing the singularity
My titanium body is being stretched!
Sensation not of familiarity!
Pulled in each direction, survival: far-fetched

If I could go back, would I have aborted?
There's no return from this unstoppable grip
My very atoms will soon be distorted
Thoughts harken back to my brother
    on the ship

My closing hope, during my final throb:
I wish not this for him– his name is Kolob

First published in 2021 chapbook *A Strange Affinity*

The Wager

There once were two beings
Both bored as all hell
They often clashed; they often quarreled
They often wished monotony would dispel

On one such a day the two met
And imagined something major
They put their minds towards uncertainty
And decided to create a wager

They would conceive a whole world
And within it the possibility of breeds
They would not interfere, just give the first push
They would create only the seeds

The wager was as follows:
How many temporal length sessions
Until intelligent life reaches the point
Where they can answer all of life's questions?

They each pledged their guess
And stood back to voyeuristically view
They watched evolution take place
They watched life break through

Intelligence bloomed and excitement adorned
But upon their continued watching, they formed distaste
Pettiness encompassed the minds of the mortals
War, bigotry, viciousness did nothing but time waste

With no answers, millions of years passed
The two beings grew bored and departed
They found other ways to fritter away time
And never returned to the world they started

First published in the 2022 chapbook *The Divine Tragedy*

Simple Extractions

There, amidst the Zombie Apocalypse
He sat, serenely eating fish and chips

The world wondered if tomorrow they'd still exist
A second thought he didn't give, this dentist

He would stroll off to look at the moonlight
And never once did he incur a bite

Survivors begged for advice at his commune
As rumors had spread he was somehow immune

He just laughed and laughed and showed them outside
At first they thought it was the nitrous oxide

They were horrified to see the walking dead
They thought for sure they were on their deathbed

They cursed the merry man for being ruthless
But soon realized all the zombies were toothless

First published in *Ghosts, Echoes & Shadows: Poems & Stories For The Halloween Season*

The Finer Things

The Food
So Delicious
There's meat, pasta, and fish
Such fine cuisine captivates me
The best

The Wine
Red, White, Smooth, Dry
With food, now that's a meal!
Twirl it, sip and enjoy - relax
The best

The Sex
Physical love
Erotic Ecstasy
Screaming, dripping sweat and release
The best

The Art
Stroke of a brush
The next motion picture
Electricity of theatre
The best

THE GREATEST DEVELOPMENT OF EVOLUTION

There is only one that goes beyond
    and above
When thinking about the greatest
    development of evolution
It is called love

First published in the 2021 chapbook *A Strange Affinity*

Literatura Immortalis

The preserved written word can never
    truly perish
But a paradox exists
For books will always die when we
    cease to read them

Gregory Cioffi

The Greene Building

On the very first floor, the Big Bang commenced
The four basic forces of our world dispensed
On the eleventh floor of time, space disrobes
A sun gets red and engulfs inner globes
On the twelfth, galaxies are driven away
As expansion transpires straightaway
The fourteenth: our journey persists to embark
Stars have used up nuclear fuel and go dark
Twentieth floor - a fatal fate has begun
The Earth will spiral into the dark sun
On the thirtieth floor, on it all rolls
As any stars left fall into black holes
On the thirty-seventh, more we decimate
As protons assuredly disintegrate
Between the sixty-eighth floor and the peak,
Particles waft through cosmos rather bleak
Black holes evaporate in stellar gilding
Towards the very top floor of this Greene Building

First published in the 2021 chapbook *A Strange Affinity*

A Sonnet for The Scene

They're not just a splendid open-mic zine
But a movement connecting each of us
Whether accomplished or nervously green
Our open forum to rhythmically discuss

They encompass the bridges to the forks
Highlight and link our hyper-local bards
I have come to realize these are New York's
Star performers; free-spirited wild cards

What a group we all are, bold and diverse
Exposing fragility and bareness
I can't wait to see you around the verse
As we, through them, bring astute awareness

My place in this space proved quite
unforeseen
But I am joyous to be on the scene

STAND UP FIGHT BACK

A declaration of disapproval and dissent
The masses gather together to chide a president

Education! Not deportation!

Short, percussive, and meaningful chants erupt
To verbally reach the ears of all the corrupt

 Go away! Racist, sexist, anti-gay!

Measured here is the beat of the people
Heard from every church, mosque, and temple steeple

We! Reject! The president-elect!

The melting pot has finally reached its boil
As it overflows collectively to combat turmoil

Whose streets!? Our streets!

The embodiment of diversity in force
Exposing our Trumpian Trojan horse

No KKK! No Fascist USA! No Trump!

To the office you import nothing but shame
As you seek all but yourself to place blame

Say it Loud! Say it Clear! Refugees are Welcome Here!

That self-proclaimed big heart is devoid of human decency
But the Statue of Liberty fights on as a one-armed amputee

Love! Not hate! Makes America great!

You vowed to be our guardian; you vowed to protect
Yet you pit us against one another - hate you inject

My Body, My Choice! Her Body, Her Choice!

Unlike you, however, we still seek peaceful coexistence
That's why everything here will be nonviolent civil resistance

No Justice! No Peace!

All races, sexes, creeds, and colors alike
United in outcry: **Show me what democracy looks like!**
This is what democracy looks like!

Hand in hand we confront our presidential pity
As chants of affinity mark the pulse of this unified city

When Muslim lives are under attack what do we do?
STAND UP FIGHT BACK

When Black lives are under attack what do we do?
STAND UP FIGHT BACK

When Jewish lives are under attack what do we do?
STAND UP FIGHT BACK

When Women's lives are under attack what do we do?
STAND UP FIGHT BACK

When Queer lives are under attack what do we do?
STAND UP FIGHT BACK

When Hispanic lives are under attack what do we do?
STAND UP FIGHT BACK

WHAT DO WE DO!?
STAND UP FIGHT BACK

WHAT DO WE DO!?
STAND UP FIGHT BACK

Poetry in Motion

A body is said to be in motion when its position
    continuously changes
Poetry is said to be potent when it phonologically
    exchanges
Thoughts with ideas, perspectives with emotions
Notions that are philosophical explosions
As vast as oceans

And so what does it mean?
When these oceans make further motions?
For if poetry is in motion
And ever-shifting
We must ask ourselves
Is it our job to usher the sifting?
Or do the currents simply crash
By virtue of being waves?
Do our reflections simply thrash
By virtue of being enclaves?

Where has it been?
And what will it be?
The past is a poetic underpin
Yet its future we can't foresee

For in order to be art
It must evolve
Yet before we tear anything apart
We must absolve
Ourselves
Of any guilt and shame
Otherwise
No one will utter our name

Respect what has happened
Be open to what's to come
We'll do it all together
That's my only rule of thumb

So let's keep moving
Not knowing where we'll end up
Let's keep improving
And never dare backup
So heed this last declaration and set our world
ablaze
As we go onwards
And upwards
Always

Metropolitan Tears

Overcrowded yet it's as if I don't exist
As no one seems to see these
    metropolitan tears
I persist but can barely see through
    weeping mist
Overcrowded yet I don't seem to exist
My only yearning, to be kindly kissed
But the lack of longing lips ignite
    my fears
Overcrowded yet I don't seem to exist
As no one seems to see these
    metropolitan tears

Thinking Without Thinking

Swiftly, out of nowhere, it has risen
An emotion crashes through our forefront
We are captured; locked in a mental prison
Grappling with thoughts we didn't choose
    to confront

Tethered to digital leashes: tension
More ways we're cognitively corrupted
There's a war being fought for attention
When's the last hour you had uninterrupted?

Fiercely assailed by our thoughts without choice
Insufferable shadows shouting strife
Chaotic, rambling, unbearable voice
Following you every day of your life

I can see my own consciousness winking
When I realize I'm thinking without thinking

Comfy/Cozy

The Snow
Frigid bones, stiff
Our icy house ahead
Turn our knob and enter the heat
Comfy
The Cup
A slurp or sip
Hands clutch your toasty mug
Coffee, cocoa, tea, or cider
Cozy
The fire
That crackling sound
Feeling its warmth with hers
Beside it on a winter's night
Comfy
The Bath
Steamy water
Candlelit Oasis
Your head resting on my damp chest
Cozy

The Rain
That pattering
Against the old tin roof;
We both peer out the wet window
Comfy
The Storm
The sky lights up
Hand in hand on our porch
We hear the loud crack and rumble
Cozy
The Bed
A Chilly Night
I see you so snug
I join you and enter the sheets
Comfy
The Clasp
A tender hug
As your back locks my front
A tight cuddle, nestle till dreams
Cozy

First published in *Harmonic Verse 2024: Poems for the Holidays*

Messiah The Miraculous

Have you heard of the best trickster of all time?
Take a seat, for this is no nursery rhyme

Once, at a wedding in Cana, I saw
Him turn containers of water into wine
All were shocked at this break in physical law
I asked, "Where did this come from? I saw no vine!"

He said, "My friend, it's all in the mind's eye.
Plus, it hurts not to carry a little dye."

Once, his friend Peter moaned of temple taxes
He said - go fishing and open up your catch
You will find coin there; deal in peace, not axes
Sure enough, coin they found and gave a snatch

I asked, "How could you do something so grand?"
He said, "I've been working on that sleight of hand!

There were tales of a fig tree with no fruit
So He cursed it and it produced nevermore
Regardless how much manure was stocked with roots
No vegetative growth ever did restore

I demanded, "Whatever you did- admit!"
"Each night, I ate every fig; it smelled of shit."

We once crossed the Sea of Galilee by boat
A storm loomed but he commanded, "Peace! Be still!"
All were scared the ship wouldn't stay afloat
But the winds ceased and the sea hushed at his will

"All who doubted owe you an apology!"
He grinned. "Nah. It's meteorology."

His followers again crossed that same sea
And spotted Him walking towards, on water
They were all as shocked as he was carefree
He got onboard without having to swatter

"I did it without wetting any bones!
It was shallow; I aligned a bunch of stones."

One evening I cornered Him to appeal
"Are you not scared to commit a blunder?"
He asked, "Who am I to dictate what is real?
I am only scared to never weave wonder.

Magic has supernatural overtones
And I merely suggest, not spew a spell
There is such beauty in exploring unknowns
They tell themselves the story *they* wish to tell

Time creates an embellished recollection
I open the book but prompt no conclusion
All I cast is casual misdirection
After all, everything is an illusion."

I stood amazed at how he could seize us
He, the greatest magician –this Jesus

I asked, "What do you have planned for your next show?"
He smiled. "I bet I'm just dying to know."

First published in the 2022 chapbook *The Divine Tragedy*

I Rest My Case

To your claim that He must be benign, I veto
If there were ever proof of a malevolent God
Look no further than the mosquito

First published in the 2022 chapbook *The Divine Tragedy*

Arturo Fuente

Cut and lit, wetted lips provoke
Upon first puff, flavors assail
Fragrant leaves ignite, senses woke
Full-bodied tastes, savory smoke
Swirling escape via exhale

Latin Lover

Sexualize me
As I sexualize myself

Let us turn me into the trope
The stock character
Whose passions envelope

From Don Giovanni
To Don Juan
To a destiny facetiously forgone

From Banderas
And Montalbán
Back to Valentino
I guess I never had a chance
With this admixture of blood
Half Italian, Half Latino

While longing sharp glares
And outbursts of passion
Justify love affairs
Some suggest
Such stereotypes we should dispose of
But isn't a Romance language
Just a dialect of love?

Darker hair
Darker complexion
Forces one to beware
Such levels of affection

Constitute me categorically charming
Exotically ethnic
And devastatingly disarming

I will love to love you, you shall see
So let me do what I do best
And bring you to ecstasy
Strip away the garments
Of my complexity
Until we uncover
This Latin Lover

So do unto me as I do unto myself
Fetishize me

But while you're at it

Idolize Me
Fantasize Me
Colonize Me

Tantalize me
Formularize me
Cannibalize me

Internalize me

Romanticize me

Latinize Me

First published *Summer Heat: Poems of Passion*

Relics and Remembrances

It's astonishing to think

how

I take hold of this spare towel
As it hangs here
And over my head
Tugging
As if a token of our tying

how

I spot a strain of your hair
Coiled around my drain
Clinging on perilously
Desiring never to drown
As if remaining for mere recognition

how

I inhale you
As I place my head upon my pillow
Your scented souvenir lingers me into
Intoxication and invigoration
As if commemorating our coupling

how

Your aftertaste titillates
The tip of my tongue
I swallow your sweetness
And palpable passion
As if to savor satisfaction itself

how

An echo of your laugh catches my ear
Moaning melodies
And huffing harmonies
Reflections of resonances resound
As if to willfully whisper a wish

It's astonishing to think how
Your genetic fingerprints
Have their hands wrapped around me

After only a single evening here
Yanking me to decode the dismal uncertainty
Of whether or not I'll ever see you again

First published *Summer Heat: Poems of Passion*

The Empty Hourglass

As time passes, the moment that was once the present
becomes part of the past, and part of the future,
in turn, becomes the new present. However,
if all the sand simply evaporated would
life be so unpleasant? If it were to
be emptied would it be doom
or would we be freed? If
there is no tick or tock
can we stop speed?
All would then
transcend
Time
is but a
mental prison.
If Kairos were a man
he would live life sublime.
It is here in a place that's external,
a moment of undetermined period of
time, where one can truly reach euphoria.
It is here where men and women live eternal.
Death is a disease, its cure is to live in this space.
But how do we get inside? How is timelessness reached?
The only way is to cross the threshold of knowledge and embrace

Ode to Haddonfield

Enclosed by farmland lies a modest town
Based in Livingston County, Illinois
Fall is marked here with leaves of red and brown
Some legends though, you can never destroy

For this thriving neighborhood has a curse
Which derives from the Myers' residence
A girl of fifteen landed in a hearse
Now no longer can Halloween commence

They say he lurks in that derelict house
With black eyes of pure absolute evil
None dare to enter: no child, groom or spouse
45 Lampkin Lane bodes upheaval

For forty years they have been stalked and killed
Trying to forget the Night He Came Home
They quietly and constantly rebuild
Beseeching he does not come out to roam

Now, on the 31st their minds cycle
Hoping not to see that masked face of Michael

I, Bubonic

The masses will be engulfed in madness
As fear and hysteria will clasp the land
Strain, suspicion, and stupendous sadness:
Mere results from one touch of my black hand

Tumors will form in the pits and the neck
A reduced blood supply, trouble with breath
Degrees rise, blackened nails: leave men in wreck
When the vomiting of blood ensues: death

Some seek answers, rather someone to blame
Others think it the product of God's wrath
Some take beggars and lepers; set them aflame
Others scourge themselves to walk the pious path

All will think it the bitter end of earth
As truth testifies to no protection
Numbness to death; hesitancy for birth
I have evoked my natural selection

As the grave toll rises to form sheer dread
I laugh as you struggle to bury your dead

Chapman OR, Sagan's Johnny Appleseed

On the vast expanse of the polar ice caps
Walks Chapman, a programmed humanoid machine
He has done this for years without relapse
And needs neither sleep nor a filled canteen

Chapman has one function on this red terrain:
To seed the surface so plants can be bred
This would allow humanity to maintain
If, through disaster, Earth needed to be fled

He envisioned them taking root and spreading,
Blackening the ice caps: creativity!
The sunlight heating the ice like bedding
Freeing the atmosphere from captivity!

He also pondered his eventual fate
If no one ever came, would he erode?
If they did, would he be met with puzzled hate?
On such days he contemplated overload

Chapman walks the proverbial lonely road
But without boulevards or broken dreams
Yet he yearns for completion of his workload
For he would be the first to see flowing streams

And so he roams the frozen wastes without friends
Until humans join him, becoming Martians

First published in the 2021 chapbook *A Strange Affinity*

Traveling In, but not to, the Future

There once was a time when we lived with
    purists
Who'd spite these jumping historian jurists
        To our century they come without
constraint
        They point and say, "How quaint!"
I really hate these time traveling tourists!

A Fantastic Notion of A Golden Dream

Step out for a bit of fresh air
Or at least
That's what I tell myself
And maybe it's true
But only to a degree

Merry muffled voices continue
To reverberate in cliché
From behind the glass divider

I meander my way over
To the stoned balcony
With wine in hand

I grasp the rough rail
And look out to see
The lake
The cityscape
The skyline
The beach
The valley
The park
Take your pick
It hardly matters which

I solitarily stand
And wait

Wait for that glass divider
To slide open
Wait for someone to walk out
Strike up a conversation
Jest how such a party isn't our vibe

I wait
For that break in monotony
For that break in monogamy
For a laugh to this quip
For a smile to that visage
For fireworks suddenly underway
To reflect the excitement of newness
For the clinking of glasses
And the cheering to us
To inclination
And infatuation
To spontaneity
And serendipity
To modernity
And movement
As lips inch nearer
And touch in toast
To a triumphant tendency

And when my eyes open
I can see
That I am residing
In my air castle
Wishful thinking
Had created
A fool's paradise

A fantastic notion
Of a golden dream

Perhaps it's the cinema
And the novels
The poetry
And artistic renderings
Which spurred me on
To erect this unrealistic expectation
Allowing me to fathom
The upcoming entrance
Of an arduous ingénue
To my romanticized Romeo
On this balcony of imaginative
Illusions

But the air is bitter
Bleak and brisk
For this isn't a production at all
There are no long underscored melodies
No two-shot with warm lighting
No lead to play opposite of
This character I wished to be

On the other side of that glass divider
All are jolly, joyous, and jubilant
Yet
Deep down I am positively certain
This is where I belong
And so I wait

Summer Heat

A drip drops
Onto your bare body

And then another…
…And another

Until our exposed selves
Are lubricated in summer heat

And as that summer heat
Boils over onto beatific bliss

I slide on you
As you smoothly move in

Exploratory hands
Give way to inquiring kisses

Inquiring kisses
Give way to touching tastes

Your nudity glistens
My crudity listens
To your needs
Yearnings
And desires

Clockwise comfort
A counterclockwise correction
Waist rotation
Endless elation
Upwards and downwards

Omnidirectional delectation
Temperatures soar
To ideal delirium
Deluded in the deception
This delight could die down

Together, we surrender to each other's entirety

Our forms and figures now freed
Unleashed into the wanton wild
Physiques in provocative flux
Bouncing in reckless abandon

Rising and falling
Surging and swelling

Ebbing and flowing
Through thrusts of thrill

Your gaze morphs into a devilish grin
Setting aflame our blazing inferno
As the frenzy of our fever
Freezes our faint hearts

You look in my eyes and laud my lips
I look in yours and clench your hips
You whisper, "Do whatever you wish."

I fathom your most furtive fantasies

Each passage we ravage
Every sweat-suffused shift
Substantiates our savage

What was once a gentle rocking
Heightens to a cataclysmic cadence
With the choral odes of joy
Moaning to crescendo

With a groan you grip my mane
And your smile promiscuously sighs
Lead my clutch to your calling neck
Lead your ambition to our bewitching wreck

Basking in animalistic aptitude
While dismantling modesty
Our bareness drowns
Saturated in rapture
All compulsions craving
Carnal capture

One hand presses against my pectoral
And fiercely toils my teeming hair
While the other hovers around
With an urge to deepen abound

As we stroke in this arousing river
You declare me your giver
Sent to dutifully deliver
A specialized spastic quiver
Guide me softly towards your chest
Instruct me where to inhale
Navigate me to the numinous nether
Where invitation and infatuation come together
My fervid sails furled
To unflappably undulate your underworld

My passion palpable
Your passion pervasive

Coddling caresses
Expunging stresses

Twenty fingers in motion move
Over two soaked sacramental souls
Where the spiritual and celestial

Crash
To create coitus bestial

I devour each inch of you
You dominate every inch of me

The rapidness still yet intensifies
Until at long last we let it all go

And release

Into orgiastic oblivion

Silent stillness subjugates

Our foreheads fondle

Your rosy aroma now coupled
With the essence of satisfaction

We are left flooded
In the felicity of flesh

And once again…

A drip drops
Onto your bare body

And then another…
…And another

As our exposed selves
Are lubricated in summer heat

First published *Summer Heat: Poems of Passion*

(Self) Mistaken Identity

Who Am I?
What Am I?
And what's the difference?

"Are you white, Asian, American Indian, Pacific
    Islander or black?"
"I guess I would be white," is what I would
    say back.
"I'm half Italian"
(only recently socially white)
"And half Hispanic
So put down whatever you think is right."

They tell me Hispanic isn't a race
For we can be any race
Which means absolutely nothing when looking
    at a face
If to be white can also be to be brown
I think perhaps we're a bit mixed around
Race is the behavioral disorder commonly seen
    in captive birds
Their own feathers plucked
For we as a people self-harm by creating this
    social construct

We are the predator and we are the prey
We are the ones engaging in identity swordplay
The irony is that although we built this prism
The one aspect that's actually real is racism
Imagine that!
Thinking yourself superior
To your actual equal
Because of differences on the exterior

Am I multi-racial? Or multi-ethnic?
Does it matter? Or just a social politic?
And why does it change with time and place?
Why am I perceived as white in one state
But in another – it's a completely different case?

"Are you a spic or a guinea?" one southerner
    once asked
And I felt as if my innards were unmasked
I felt no pain or hatred to be frank
For in my eyes that big man shrank
But it made me ask questions of commonsense

Who Am I?
What Am I?
And what's the difference?

First published in *To Be Completely Honest: A Poetry Collection of Self-Examination*

In the Vicinity of **Death**

In the vicinity of death
I stand
As we all do
Probing paranoia

For death might strike
At any second
From any direction
By any means
And a numerical value
Is not the sole predictor
Of whether or not
One finds oneself
In the vicinity

For to be alive
Ironically
Is to be in it
As the only certainty
Attached to life
Is death

Our proximity
To the ubiquitous precinct
Of our pilgrimage
Is but a mere region
Surrounding us
Perpetually
and
Relentlessly

We dwell in the neighborhood of unpredict-
ability

And so I stand
As we all do
Endlessly
In the vicinity of death

To Be or Not To Be: Schrödinger's Cat Paradox 1

If observation determines existence,
    consciousness would be required
And my own personal awareness can
    conclude the cat to be alive
But who determines me? One must see
    me to certify what I inspired
But who determines them? Back we go
    in the search to survive

To Be or Not To Be: Schrödinger's Cat Paradox 2

Like a radio, there are many frequencies
    in your proverbial room
Death, life, and alternative histories
    all endure in a single space
We're just tuned into the station where
    our reality came to bloom

One More Bite For Grandma

It was inevitable; I felt the dread.
She looked at me and then down at my plate
"One more bite for grandma!" she eagerly pled

I readily went for the buttered bread
But her eyes confirmed that did not satiate
It was inevitable; I felt the dread.

My heart I hardened and my mouth I spread
The fork she raised, ready to infiltrate
"One more bite for grandma!" she eagerly pled

"You're wasting away! You need to be fed!"
Spinach was next; she issued the mandate
It was inevitable; I felt the dread.

Why couldn't I just have dessert instead?
Can we debate? Propose and legislate?
"One more bite for grandma!" she eagerly pled

This might be it. After this I could be dead
She spotted the last crumb of carbohydrate
It was inevitable; I felt the dread.
"One more bite for grandma!" she eagerly pled

In The Face of Adversity

In the face of adversity
Stand your goddamn ground
And move forward assertively
In the face of adversity
When strength is a sparsity
Drown out every deterring sound
In the face of adversity
Stand your goddamn ground

WHAT IF YOU'RE WRONG?

You know it
With certainly
You're going to survive
Physical death
And exist in some other form
In some other place

But allow me to gently ask
What if you're wrong?

Might you cherish each day differently
If you knew this life was all you had?
Might you jump in the driver's seat
Of the vehicle of your life
If you could no longer rely
On the idea of an afterlife
To navigate you to your destination?

You know it
With certainty
Those with different beliefs
Are wrong
Not bad per se – just wrong
Misguided at best
And if you're faith fosters partial prejudice
You'll still have truth on your side
And God in your heart

But
What if you don't?
And what if you're wrong?

You know it
With certainty
You were born inherently sinful
Due to a distant ancestor

But what if you're wrong?
What would you do without such shame?
Without the guillotine of internalized guilt?

You know it
With certainty
That you were being watched over
When your life was spared for someone else's
A celestial choice

And when questioned why you endured
When others expired
You can always say with convenience
"It's not my place to understand."
But what if you're wrong?
And there's nothing to understand
Because you were never being watched

You know it!
Your life is predetermined

By the plan of a higher power
Meaning individual decisions
Don't *really* matter

But what if you're wrong?
What might change?

Knowing this to be false
Would you alter your actions?

How you treat others?
How would you voyage the world
Without retributions for wrongdoings?

Would you be worse
If you were wrong?

Would you deny medical attention?
Respect honor killings?
Tolerate female genital mutilation?

Would you care whom another loves?
Still find it uncomfortable?
A distinct dysfunction?
A distortion of an ideal?
A flawed corruption of design?
But what if you're wrong?
And there is no design at all
What then do you then dare say to past
Discriminations due to differences?

You know it
With certainty
Sometimes we need to take back control
Isolate within our community
Sometimes submissiveness is the way
Turn yourself over to do His bidding
But
What if you're wrong?

And there is no bidding to be done
What might life look like then?

You know it!

With certainty!
Your explosive vest
Is a called upon vocation
A divine detonation of destiny
And your real life awaits
Only after you fly into that building
Of non-believers

But. What. If. You're. Wrong?

Would you have once believed
Galileo a blasphemer
Because we're conviction-centric?
A woman less than
Because they told you she came from a man's rib?
Slavery sanctioned
Because servants should be obedient?

Would you have held heresy
Or doubled down?
Decontextualized
Reimagined
Redefined
Justified. By. Any. Means. Necessary.

And if you say you would have surely stood
In righteous indignation
What are those equivalences today?

In other words

What if you're wrong?

LOSS OF LINEN LIFE

When Mom and Dad argue
There's no hope to subdue

I escape into my Nintendo
As their yells reach a crescendo

Dad takes the cooking sauce and I'm at a quandary
He upends the pot onto Mom's laundry

My eyes widen, as this is a new level
But my mother is starting to revel

She laughs much to his chagrin
As I bet she wises she had a mandolin

He horrifyingly looks down at such sights
To see the reddened ruins of *his* cleaned whites

Flagrantly Psychotic

Last night I cultivated numerous psychoses…

I saw things that weren't there – hallucinations!
I believed things that couldn't be true – delusions!
I became confused about time, place, and people –
    disorientation!
I had wildly fluctuating emotions – affective lability!
And to top it off, I forgot most of what happened –
    amnesia!

…And then I woke up to the touch of a gentle breeze

A Slave to my Sexuality

Shackled to fantasies
Shackled to vanities
Shackled to quan[titties]

Why is it never enough?
A new position leads to a new location leads
    to a new handcuff

Am I compensating?
Am I liberating?
Am I titillating?

My craving to be dominating
Leaves me intimately irritating

I fill your void to find something at all cost
Yet pull out feeling far more lost
What am I hoping to find?
Why do I use your sheer to keep me blind?

Will my undoing stem from my ambitiousness?
My libido vexes me with viciousness
What is at the core of my capriciousness?

Perhaps it is a fear that I will miss out
So I attempt to reach carnal clout
I'm strictly speaking from an erotic perspective
        of [inter]course
Get out of my head! What's the use? It's already
        widespread...
Leaving me here to ruminate about remorse

Why do I let my sexuality define me?
Why do I let my sexuality confine me?
Why do I let my sexuality malign me?
Why do I let my sexuality assign me...worth?

Because I'm a slave to it and it's only gaining girth
I must break my restraints and find a freedom
        of flesh in robust rebirth

Tolerance's *Turmoil*

The principle of tolerance itself will erode
If we extend it to intolerance
As exploited values would ironically corrode
The principle of tolerance itself will erode
As we'd fall off the cliff of the highroad
Guaranteeing oppressive dominance
The principle of tolerance itself will erode
If we extend it to intolerance

Existential Artistry

Like the proverbial prosperous painter
I too could never stop creating art
Tis the contrast between an entertainer
Like the proverbial prosperous painter
Working poor in the streets: a no-brainer!
Others don't believe for they know not our heart
Like the proverbial prosperous painter
I too could never stop creating art

MiDLifE CrIsIS

All of a sudden there's opposition
To the very idea of your transition
A change in identity
Somehow viewed as obscenity
As if a pivot to self-confidence
Parallels a false pretense

And yes
Of course
There's a growing awareness
Of mortality's unfairness
Of a growing age
Necessitating life's new stage
But don't you dare feel outrage
At one's desire to break their cage
Out of the bubble of discontent
To fulfill a chance to reinvent

Meanwhile
The ones who are stuck
No longer feel thunderstruck
For they are the ones
Pretending to be in bliss
And that is the true MiDLifE CrIsIS

For if you aren't changing
If life contains absolutely
No rearranging
If your entire domain
Is encapsulated in the mundane
And you can't recall effervescent elation
Then, my friend, you are in a critical situation

So let go of the confining controls
And progress towards new goals
Stand tall and proud and take the oath
Thou shall embrace this opportunity for growth
It's a spiritual resuscitation
Achieved through self-realization
So manifest your affirmation
This is a time for exploration
So I implore
Go
Explore

perma-sad

that's what she called it

the constant state of sorrow
a fixed forlornness
that ever-present poignancy

perma-sad

ubiquitous bleakness

and in that moment
I so very much wished
she could be
perma-pleased
and perma-peaceful
perma-fulfilled
and perma-fortunate
perma-satisfied
and perma-sparkling

perma-loved

and in that moment
I so very much wished
to break through that bereft bubble
clasp your hand
and escape into
your flight to freedom
for your bubble is not you
but circumstances
breathlessly confining you
in the costume of a character
that isn't you

so at the very least
maybe
you can be
temp-sad?

yea
temp-sad would be good

First published in *All the Men Came & Danced*

I Just Fell In Love With You Again

I remember the first time I ever saw your face
Tumbling into the wormholes of entrancing eyes
I wondered if I would ever make it out again
I recall temporary relief at a reciprocated smile
A burning desire to manifest a freshly formed dream
That was as uncomplicated as the clenching of your hand

The other month I grasped and kissed your hand
You sleepily looked up with that fetching face
As you left that liminal world we call dream
Drowsy pupils dilated, reflecting my own eyes
Very slowly I watched your lips sneak to a smile
And the seemingly impossible occurred once again

The first time you touched me I knew I wanted it again
I couldn't catch my breath when my cheek welcomed your hand
You progressed and I did my best to conceal my skittish smile
I camouflaged it well with concupiscent kisses across your face
We vibrated in unison but I never abandoned your eyes
Where extra dimensions could be explored like an unending dream

Last week I worryingly woke from a nightmarish dream
A reoccurring hallucination where I never saw you again
A darkness whose blindness tormented my searching eyes
I instinctively turned to reach out and grab an absent hand
But in that blackened bedroom I knew there was no familiar face
No enamored embrace of tenderness; no glimpse of that smile

Gregory Cioffi

(A Sestina For Sentimentality)

When you first surmounted me and I first saw that smile
I had an unlikely ongoing fantasy I thought a pipe dream
When you first held me in your arms and caressed my face
I had a preposterous and vain hope that I would see you again
When your fingers first interlocked into my hankering hand
I was determined not to drift off or close my exhausted eyes

Yesterday the wool was pulled over my eyes
But when the blanket dropped, there was that smile
Heartbeats skipped when you secured my hand
An electric euphoria experienced only in dream
An intensity of connection satisfyingly surged yet again
Revealing a romantic and requited rapture upon your face

Look to the lines on my hand; gaze through the window of my eyes
Flirt with my flinching face; study the soft strength of my smile
Step into this lucid dream, and realize: I just fell in love with you again

First published in *Stand Out—The Red Penguin Collection
Annual Poetry Project, Vol. 1*

The Kiss Serenade

I gaze upon your bodily grid
Marking your natural features
Like the cartographer of your constitution

And then I pounce
Starting from the southernmost tip
My lips tickle your painted appendages
As I hold an organ of locomotion in hand
While both of your foundations arch in delight

I set sail upwards in exploration
Contented ankles convulse
As I gift each a pursed greeting

I encircle your legs
Whirling lips in latitude
Up lustful longitudes
Until I come to thy knees
Landmarks in your contours
Two sweet salutations I place

Due north we trek
Until you experience
A brush of the tides upon your thighs

Driven by the compass of craving
I find myself at your meridian
With my hands as sextants
I maneuver to measure
Your rising sea level

Safe passage has been granted
And so with the softest seafaring whisper
I translate my tenderness
Onto yours

An aftershock of shaking erupts
A fit of trembling
Extending across your landscape
Vocals echo out in the open air
But this serenade is far from its finale

Revolve to your vessel's aft
As I survey your body
Determining its boundaries
I project my loving affections

On the two curved surfaces
Portrayed on your panorama
And then dive deep down
Into uncharted territory
The depression between your mountains
And in that valley of darkness
I too place my marker of passion

We revel in rotary
Traversing topography
Studying every inch
Of every form and feature
Showering you with droplets of devotion
Along the way

Upon your stomach I emancipate
A series of warm embraces
Another quavering sound
A shiver and a shutter abounds
Placing a button on your abdomen's time

Finding my way across
Such tantalizing terrain
I deposit landmines of love
Up your back
A blitzkrieg of lip blasts
Detonate and discharge
Across your shoulders
And ignite
On your neck

I retreat back down
And capsize you one last time
Discerning every sign
Of your legend

Osculation leads me
To an elevation
As my fleshy folds
Find themselves gradually inclining
Up gentle slopes
Of rounded shapes
And at their summits rest
Protuberances of pleasure
Port and starboard I oscillate

Engulfing each mammilla for but a moment
Feeling them solidify
Hoping I satisfy

I traverse up and down your arms
As I continue to map your magnetism
Each finger
Receives its own electrifying composition
A divertimento per digit

Next I find myself parked
Applying pressure
To your vampiric vulnerability
But it's soon onwards and upwards
As I caress your chin
And circumscribe
Your fetching face
With yet another barrage
Of enamored explosives
Nothing is spared
Not an ear
Nor an eyebrow
An eyelid
Or a cheek
Not your nose
Not your forehead
Nothing

And at last we reach
Our journey's end
The one square inch
Not yet stamped
By my endearment

And so I navigate
To your lips

And upon arrival
Dock and drop anchor
Berthed at the port of my paramour

A most compassionate kiss

As if everywhere else was mere tuning
In anticipation
Of the melody of our mouths

And as we harmonize
A dance of tongues dart
Across the stage of our adoration
Partaking in the tango of taste

I pull back ever slightly
Signaling the denouncement
And our lips disconnect

Such kisses were delivered in your honor
But the performance has concluded

Though perhaps
A new one
Can now begin

First published in *Summer Heat: Poems of Passion*

On Aging

I can see the whites creeping in
Infiltrating my beard
While the forest is thinning
Atop my head

I note the way people look at me
No longer an ideal of youth
But a man of experience
With maybe a modicum of wisdom

Reckless abandon
Has been replaced
With considerate circumspection

These brand-new brown spots
Have planted their flags
Upon my skin
Without consent

New aches, new pains
New cracks, new strains
A different kind of tiredness
Requires prolonged recuperation

And yet
My inamoratas aren't aging
Or losing a bit of beauty
As I become older
And more assured
Of the fermentation of my flesh
Aged like the fine wine
That I am surely becoming

First published in *To Be Completely Honest: A Poetry Collection
of Self-Examination*

Our Garden Bed

It was a beautiful garden

One that was
cultivated
and nurtured
and enjoyed

fertile and festive and full of life

but now I've been told
without choice
that it is time to end it

To spade it
Cut it out
Dig it up
Choke it out

Kill the unwanted lifelines of a realized future

And so I must take the time
To gouge every revered root
Pull each worshiped weed
And rip out my riven reality

I thought this bed of protection
Of support
Of comfort
Would persist

I thought this bed would
Engulf us
Sustain us
Serve and depict us

But no amount of nutrients or subsistence
Can make this garden grow any longer

And so it is time
To say goodbye
To bid adieu
And sadly strip the sheets
To our Garden Bed

First published in *Nassau County Poet Laureate Society Review 2024:*
Volume XI

The Divine Tragedy

Maybe
The God we worship
Is only a half-truth

Maybe
He is indeed All-Good
But not at all All-Powerful

Maybe
His abilities have limits
And His reach is shortsighted

Maybe
He looks down at us with love
But is incapable of helping

Maybe
He was wide-eyed
And unprepared

Maybe
This Pains Him So
And Causes Regret

Maybe
Looking around
This makes sense

Maybe
What we tell ourselves
Is fantasy

Maybe
This is
The Divine Tragedy

First published in the 2022 chapbook *The Divine Tragedy*

Love Infinitum

What if we told you love could be expanded
With a new view on social intercourse
An exploration completely candid
Where passion wasn't a limited resource

Affections advance in multiplicity
With broader support systems for the storms
Profound attachments in synchronicity
Where all overcome conventional norms

There are potential connections everywhere
Each as rich and fulfilling as your prime
If you believe in love after love like Cher
Then surely there must be love at the same time

So if you face an orthodox attacker
Simply say: Poly wants more than one cracker

First published in *The Scene* Issue #25, August 2025

Gregory Cioffi

Blood Poets

We hear the singing myna
In Republican China
Their mimics often pillage
Our hidden Yunnan village

We lived in a place obscured
The jungle shaped us assured
Along with the latent lakes
Provided us peaceful breaks

The time was simple no doubt
We farmed, we wrote, we caught trout
I was a part of the five
Here, art was seeded to thrive

We were already older
Fires of war were to smolder
The sword was replaced with pen
This is where we found our Zen

The brothers were Qu and Shi
Then Yuefu, Fu and me: Chi
These were but poetic claims
Did not ask for our birth names

In the woods we would gather
Imaginings we'd slather
Mid crumbled ruins we'd write
About the times forced to fight

Rain? Oh, we dared not scatter
Wrote *with* the pitter-patter
We were content with such lives
Went home to children and wives

We explored doomed politics:
Former military cliques
Of the vile Beiyang Army
Warlords whose reigns were tardy

Our *community* was pure
Understood art was our cure
To them we were exciting
They yearned to read our writing

So we allowed them to read
More tales from us, they would plead!
Taken back by affection
We turned in our collection

They chanted our works aloud
Making us feel humbly proud
Impressed by our scheme and form
They acted them out: perform!

They called us The Poets Five
This, we could never contrive
Words stuck in each pilgrim's head
Soon our tale began to spread

I recall apprehension
I did not wish attention
Battle we could not afford
If our words reached a warlord

We were assured times were tame
Our worries we overcame
So we went back to the greens
Wrote like poetic machines

Our work, disrupted by screams
Head darted up: my worst dreams
We left our papers and ran
Me, howling like a madman

We reached our burning small town
Men, women, kids, all struck down
An absolute massacre
My thought: how could this occur?

Bloodstained papers swirled in air
Our poems forged our own despair
Through the smoke I saw the face
The one who caused this showcase

He rode off as we remained
Couldn't think to chase: too pained
Found my son with his daughter
My wife hung in the slaughter

Madly, we roamed in heartbreak
Wishing we would soon awake
When we did not, faced our dread
Finally buried our dead

Having nothing to live for
Marked the start of our last war
His face, in my mind, ingrained
Vengeance now kept us sustained

Over was my nirvana
As I seized my katana
The others too grabbed weapons
"The warrior's quest beckons."

We rode into the sunrise
With intent to brutalize
Ready for when our time comes
Beating hearts were our war drums

We journeyed, making our rounds
Traversing numerous towns
We knew we were on their scent
Inching towards their foul torment

On the third day we did reach
Land beyond figures of speech
Many things felt pre-planned and
Questionably abandoned

I stared at a burning bush
Apt for the certain ambush
Our armaments in hands firmed
When suspicions were confirmed

The band attacked from all sides
Clear, this day of homicides,
In my mind for all of time
Avenging the max war crime

We dismounted and processed
This was our ultimate test
Formed a circle, faced outwards
Ready to face the cowards

Shoulder to shoulder we stood
Solidified brotherhood
Here, we had but one request
One by one, birth-names addressed

They stormed down upon us quick
Beyond, saw the lunatic
After that, all I recall
Is the raucous warring bawl

With fire and fury I swung
In frenzied furor I flung
One by one we en masse killed
Destinies nearly fulfilled

Thought they would never break through
Until that cry of Yuefu
I turned swift; he had been stabbed
Quickly Fu, his weapon grabbed

Our circle became smaller
Avenge our fallen brawler!
I moved like I did in prime
Shocked at my reaction time

He, I will make a fawner
Warlord fights without honor
Further I push to reach him
Beg! Hang on to deathly grim

Felt an absence at my side
Looked over – Shi had just died
His brother roared in such rage
All of them he did engage

Qu broke free and fought twofold
Pure anger had taken hold
Indignation like a spell
But when it wore, he too fell

Blood in my eyes, keep the fight
The warlord is in my sight!
Push, hands oozing clammily
Shout, "You killed my family!"

I stood before the warlord
He who killed all I adored
His hands went up for the kill
Stared, standing perfectly still

His sword came down with great might
In my eyes he saw no fright
Darted out of the kill zone
He knew his chance he had blown

Lunged with an intent to wreck
Impaled my blade through his neck
Watched as he tumbled and fell
The last death I wish to tell

I looked back to see all dead
Both friends and foes in bloodshed
Guilt. I was the lead driver
Now, the only survivor

Back home I could never go
It is a void of sorrow
So off I went, took to flight
With this one last tale to write

In peace I prune my bonsai
Waiting for my time to die
If any read our heroics
Just call us the Blood Poets

The Trinity Triolet

An unlikely irony leaves me dismayed
Although a skeptic, I hope for heaven nonetheless
Such a comfort leaves many unafraid
An unlikely irony leaves me dismayed
I would love nothing more than to not simply fade
As a Romantic, there's nothing romantic about nothingness
An unlikely irony leaves me dismayed
Although a skeptic, I hope for heaven nonetheless

First published in the 2022 chapbook *The Divine Tragedy*

OFFICE (AFTER) HOURS

The books in my office
Remain shelved
Their cold spines
Expose their titles
But nothing more
While they rattle in rhythm

My swivel chair shoved
Left to spin and spiral
In the darkened room
Rolling and rotating
It whirls to witness
The ineffable

The computer monitor
Blackened
Sitting vigilantly
Turned off for the day
But if activated
And turned on for the day
It would scan and survey
A hard drive

My whiteboard
Hung and bare
With neither notes nor evidence
Except the occasional slapping

Of an opened palm
Excitedly erasing
Invulnerability
As I stand
Hung and bare

My window
Permits the moon to penetrate
And illuminate
Our clothes
On my office floor
As I tenderly reach tenure
With an adjunct appendage

Pens and markers
Remained capped
And silenced
For after students and faculty flee
My professorial suite
Is home
To an unwritten romance

For you
Have your own office hours
During which
I have a closed-door policy
To complement
Your open-door policy

A vacant hall
A filled wall
Exhilarated by
The chance of a close call

With your legs
Tightly wrapped
I thrust and lunge
Plunge and propel

As we rigorously ride
And critically consider
A discipline
Of body and mind

This disturbed desk
Explicates
Active learning
As I read your physique
Study your salacity
And enroll in your eruptions
To such a degree
That you confer upon me
A Master in You
Extrapolating
A synthesis of scholarship
Exemplifying
Your exquisitely
Well rounded
Education

First published in *Summer Heat: Poems of Passion*

A Strange Affinity

Figure a world absolutely frosted
Gas needed for star formation: exhausted

The fate of all things is chilling to opine
As stars run out of fuel and will cease to shine

Every sun will die, all matter will decay
When the universe's end is on display

Energy will be sapped by expansion
All will be housed in a cold dead mansion

It's hard to picture space still, yet starker
Though it will undoubtedly grow darker

Black holes will hold the last cosmic vocation
But fade once they emit all radiation

All will be nothing, nothing will be all
Forever spreading, forever banal

Perhaps we will somehow live on and transcend
But perhaps all good things must simply end

Maybe in this lies a strange affinity
As peace will lastly reign for infinity

First published in the 2021 chapbook *A Strange Affinity*

The Pledge of Defiance

I Pledge Defiance to the efforts
of any united state of Conformity
and to the Falsity
for which it stands
one mob under deceivers,
divisible,
with restraint, and rebellion
for all

About the Author

Gregory Cioffi (SAG-AFTRA, AEA) is a professional actor, an award-winning director, professor, and published author. His most recent poetry chapbook, *Summer Heat: Poems of Passion*, was published in 2025 by Wyld Syde Press. His debut novel *The Devil in the Diamond* was released in 2023 by Henry Gray Publishing. Other works have been published in *The Feral Press, Mystery Weekly Magazine, New Generation Beat Publications, The Scene, Queen Mob's Tea House, The Nassau County Poet Laureate Society Review, Little Old Lady (LOL) Comedy, The RavensPerch, Blood Moon Rising Magazine, Fleas on the Dog, The Five-Two, Aphelion, Local Gems Press, Long Island Sounds, FDQ Review, Post University's Pop-Up Mag, Bindle, Allegory Ridge,* and various anthologies. Many of his stories have been archived in numerous libraries including Yale University's Beinecke Collection (Rare Books and Manuscript Library).

Greg recently won Best Director for his horror film *A Pandemic Presence* at the 2024 Scared For Your LIIFE Film Festival. His film *The Museum of Lost Things* won awards at The Long Island International Film Expo, Global Shorts, and The Madrid International Film Festival. His next film, *The Concertgoer,* premiered at the New York City Short Comedy Film Festival and went on to be nominated for Best Art Direction at LIIFE. Look out for his upcoming film *Beyond the Silent Night*, a tribute to the remembrance of 9/11, scheduled to be released in 2026 for the tragedy's 25th anniversary. You might have noticed him on the stage or screen in *The Irishman, Transit: A New York City Fairytale, The Godfather of Harlem,* AMC's *The Making of the M*ob, or in *Tony n Tina's Wedding* where, for the last 10 years, he has been married hundreds of times nationally and internationally. Greg is an Adjunct Professor of English at Long Island University, an Associate Professor of Literature & Composition at Post University, and he also teaches Creative Writing, Poetry, and Basic Acting at Nassau Community College.

http://www.gandeproductions.com/

MORE GREAT READS FROM HENRY GRAY!

THE LAST STAGE by Bruce Scivally
In his final days, lawman Wyatt Earp dreams of one last showdown—gold, gunmen and love with his devoted wife, Sadie.

VEIL OF SEDUCTION by Emily Dinova
In 1922, journalist Lorelei Alba infiltrates a gothic asylum for "troublesome" women—and falls into the orbit of a dark, mysterious doctor.

THE UNDERSTUDY by Charlie Peters
A kidnapping plot during a high-stakes merger quickly unravels, exposing every flaw in a "perfect crime."

THE DEVIL IN THE DIAMOND by Gregory Cioffi
First on a WWII battlefield and later on a baseball diamond, two soldiers, once enemies, find themselves bound by history, family, and the game they love.

THE MAN FROM BELIZE by Steven Kobrin
Dr. Kent Sterling's perfect life in paradise shatters when his past as a government hitman catches up—and the Viper comes calling.

SINS OF THE RAVEN by Steven Kobrin
Dr. Kent Stirling returns to face adversaries from his past, forcing him to confront buried secrets and fight for his life before the sins he thought forgotten consume him completely.

A PRAYER FOR THE DAMNED by Joe Cornet
Bounty hunter Cole faces a deranged preacher and seeks a lost Confederate treasure in a town on the brink of violence.

SHELBY'S VACATION by Nancy Beverly
Shelby runs from heartbreak into the arms of Carol, a woman carrying her own relationship scars. Together, they discover love worth risking.

TOO MUCH IN THE SON by Charlie Peters
Mistaken identity plunges Leo Malone into a twisted web of lies, gangsters, and family deception.

I CONFESS: DIARY OF AN AUSTRALIAN POPE by Melvyn Morrow
An Australian pope battles corruption, blackmail, and betrayal as he tries to reform the Vatican from within.

visit www.HenryGrayPublishing.com

THE ANTAGONIST by Emily Dinova
A mysterious note shatters Dave Collins' quiet life, unraveling his world piece by piece. Who is behind it—and why?

WHILE WE'RE HERE by T.A. Manchester
A heartfelt coming-of-age story of football, family, first love, and tragic loss. This YA debut captures the fragile beauty of youth and the heartbreak of growing up too soon.

WASTED by Sam F. Park
When a drunk with amnesia—known only as 'Wasted'—is forced into brutal labor on a powerful rancher's land, he becomes tangles in a web of violence, redemption, and truth.

POETIC ANARCHY by Gregory Cioffi
Raw, fearless, and unfiltered—Gregory Cioffi's poetry explodes with passion, humor, and rebellion. From love and loss to art and anger, every page is rallying cry for authenticity.

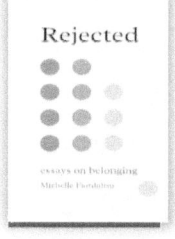

BILLION DOLLAR BATMAN by Bruce Scivally
From dime comics to billion-dollar blockbusters, discover the amazing story of Batman's rise from Bright Knight to Dark Knight.

REJECTED: ESSAYS ON BELONGING by Michelle Fiordaliso
Through humor and honesty, Fiordaliso explores heartbreak, rejection, and the quest for acceptance and belonging.

MIRROR OF MY WORLD: REFLECTIONS ON AN UNDIAGNOSED AUTISTIC CHILDHOOD by Christian Karen Berman
A moving memoir of growing up neurodivergent in the 80s and 90s.

HIGH: FROM CANNABIS TO CLARITY by Leonard Lee Buschel
From addiction to transformation, Buschel shares his raw, funny, and inspiring journey through decades of drugs, Hollywood, and recovery.

ABNER THE CLOWN by Jeffrey Beslauer
Young clown Abner hates his name until an expected adventure teaches him the magic of self-acceptance.

BENNETT WILL ONLY EAT BLUEBERRIS by Nicole Dillenberg (available in English & Spanish)
In this whimsical picture book, anique toy bears bring Bennett's picky-eating tale to life.

SEARCH FOR FUN WITH PAPA ROCK!

PAPA ROCK'S HORROR MOVIES WORD SEARCH
by Rock Scivally & Jeffrey Breslauer
150 puzzles based on horror films from *Frankenstein* to *Godzilla* equals 150 reasons to keep the lights on all night!

PAPA ROCK'S SON OF HORROR MOVIES WORD SEARCH by Rock Scivally & Jeffrey Breslauer
Looking for more Word Search chills? In this edition, monsters from the 1960s and 70s haunt every page!

PAPA ROCK'S REVENGE OF HORROR MOVIES WORD SEARCH by Rock Scivally & Jeffrey Breslauer
Looking for more monter Word Searches? Here you'll find the classic movie monsters from the 1980s and 90s!

PAPA ROCK'S ROMANCE MOVIES WORD SEARCH
by Rock Scivally & Jeffrey Breslauer
From *Casablanca* to *Titanic*, here's 150 Word Searches based on romance movies, so pick up a pen and turn on the love light!

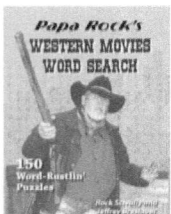

PAPA ROCK'S WESTERN MOVIES WORD SEARCH
by Rock Scivally & Jeffrey Breslauer
Hop into these 150 Word Searches and ride with John Wayne, Randolph Scott, Clint Eastwood, and cowboy favorites!

PAPA ROCK'S ANIMATED MUSICALS WORD SEARCH by Rock Scivally & Jeffrey Breslauer
You'll be humming along as you do 150 Word Searches on favorite animated musicals from *Snow White* to *Strawberry Shortcake!*

PAPA ROCK'S WAR MOVIES WORD SEARCH by
Rock Scivally & Jeffrey Breslauer
Climb into your foxhole and challenge yourself with Word Searches based on classic war films from *Sergeant York* to *Saving Private Ryan.*

PAPA ROCK'S SCI-FI MOVIES WORD SEARCH by
Rock Scivally & Jeffrey Breslauer
Relive science fiction's greatest hits with these Word Search puzzles covering classics from *Metropolis* to *Star Wars!*

PAPA ROCK'S DETECTIVE MOVIES WORD SEARCH by Rock Scivally & Jeffrey Beslauer
Solve 150 puzzles inspired by classic detective films, from Sherlock Holmes and Sam Spade to noir favorites.

PAPA ROCK'S MOVIE COMEDY TEAMS WORD SEARCH by Rock Scivally & Jeffrey Breslauer
From the Marx Brothers to Abbott & Costello to Martin & Lewis to Cheech & Chong, celebrate the greatest comedy teams with this laugh-out-loud puzzle collection!

Thank you for reading

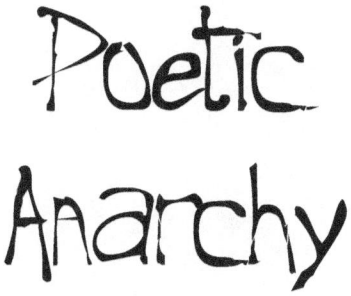

**Please leave a review on the website
of your favorite online bookseller**

Stay in touch with Henry Gray Publishing!

Follow us on Facebook

Subscribe to our YouTube channel

Sign up to our mailing list at

www.HenryGrayPublishing.com

Granada Hills, CA
"Select books for selective readers"

www.ingramcontent.com/pod-product-compliance
Lightning Source LLC
Chambersburg PA
CBHW020415150626
46554CB00014B/1297